Extending SaltStack

Extend the power of your infrastructure and applications with Salt modules

Joseph Hall

[PACKT] open source
PUBLISHING
community experience distilled

BIRMINGHAM - MUMBAI

Extending SaltStack

First published: March 2016

Production reference: 1160316

Published by Packt Publishing Ltd.
Livery Place
35 Livery Street
Birmingham B3 2PB, UK.

ISBN 978-1-78588-861-8

www.packtpub.com

Credits

Author
Joseph Hall

Reviewers
C. R. Oldham

Mike Place

Commissioning Editor
Kunal Parikh

Acquisition Editor
Reshma Raman

Content Development Editor
Merwyn D'souza

Technical Editor
Mohit Hassija

Copy Editors
Dipti Mankame

Jonathan Todd

Project Coordinator
Nikhil Nair

Proofreader
Safis Editing

Indexer
Priya Sane

Graphics
Kirk D'Penha

Production Coordinator
Shantanu N. Zagade

Cover Work
Shantanu N. Zagade

Foreword

Regardless of your current experience with Salt, you will find this book a necessary addition to unlock the full potential and capabilities of Salt to manage your infrastructure. Salt has a very flexible and modular architecture, and you will no doubt get very far down the path of fully automating your environment with the out-of-the-box Salt setup. However, we all have those custom unique quirks to our environments, or legacy systems, which require special treatment. Extending SaltStack will arm you with all of the information you need to get the most out of Salt to manage those hard-to-reach places of your environment to obtain full automation.

As the author of one of Salt's cloud modules, I can only say that I am envious of your position! I wish that this book had been available to provide the basics of module development when I was getting started. You'll find this book does a great job of covering all the basics of extending Salt, whereas also providing the detailed depth to really understand how your modules plug in with the rest of Salt.

Joseph Hall was the first engineer working at SaltStack apart from the Founder, Thomas Hatch. He has worked on all components of Salt and built much of the foundation that makes the tool so easy to extend. I have positive feelings that you'll find this book concise, easy to follow, and an outstanding resource to learn how to take full advantage of Salt. Go forth and automate!

Eric Johnson
Author of SaltStack's Google Compute Engine cloud module

About the Author

Joseph Hall has been working with SaltStack for a very long time. His first commit was on March 14, 2011, making him the second contributor to the Salt codebase. At the time his Python skills weren't very good, but writing Salt modules made them better. He has written a number of Salt modules and is planning to write many more. He has also written *Mastering SaltStack, Packt Publishing*.

I would like to thank my beautiful and wonderful wife Nat for putting up with me for two books and helping me keep my sanity. I would like to thank Merwyn D'Souza, Reshma Raman, and everyone else that I've worked with at Packt for just being so awesome. I would also like to thank Colton Meyers for introducing me to Packt, Mike Place and C. R. Oldham for providing technical review for this book, and Tom Hatch for creating this amazing piece of software.

About the Reviewer

C. R. Oldham is a platform engineer and team lead for the integrations team at SaltStack. A veteran of the technology industry, he has had his hands in almost every aspect of computing in his 20+ years' career, including software development, engineering management, systems administration, and open source. He resides in Utah with his wife, three kids, two cats, a veiled chameleon, and an albino corn snake. You can find his occasional writings at `http://ncbt.org`.

www.PacktPub.com

eBooks, discount offers, and more

Did you know that Packt offers eBook versions of every book published, with PDF and ePub files available? You can upgrade to the eBook version at www.PacktPub.com and as a print book customer, you are entitled to a discount on the eBook copy. Get in touch with us at customercare@packtpub.com for more details.

At www.PacktPub.com, you can also read a collection of free technical articles, sign up for a range of free newsletters and receive exclusive discounts and offers on Packt books and eBooks.

https://www2.packtpub.com/books/subscription/packtlib

Do you need instant solutions to your IT questions? PacktLib is Packt's online digital book library. Here, you can search, access, and read Packt's entire library of books.

Why subscribe?

- Fully searchable across every book published by Packt
- Copy and paste, print, and bookmark content
- On demand and accessible via a web browser

This book is dedicated to Nat.

"You flicker

And you're beautiful

You glow inside my head

You hold me hypnotized

I'm mesmerized"

– The Cure, *The Caterpillar*

Table of Contents

Preface

You hold in your hands (or in your e-reader) the first book dedicated to writing code to be used with the SaltStack framework of tools.

What this book covers

Chapter 1, Starting with the Basics, starts with a discussion of the two core principles that this book focuses on: how Salt uses Python and how the Loader system works. These form the foundation of extending Salt.

Chapter 2, Writing Execution Modules, explains that the heavy lifting in most of Salt is performed by execution modules, which are often wrapped by other modules. A solid understanding of execution modules will also be key to understanding how other module types work.

Chapter 3, Extending Salt Configuration, explains that the ability to dynamically manage configuration can make some modules far more useful. Some modules won't even work without dynamic configuration. Here, we explore different ways to provide that.

Chapter 4, Wrapping States Around Modules, supports the fact that execution modules make things work, but state modules make that work persist. In this chapter, you will see how to manage execution modules using state modules.

Chapter 5, Rendering Data, shows that the renderer system allows you to add your own templating systems, increasing the power of states. Jinja and YAML are all well and good, but sometimes, you need something more.

Chapter 6, Handling Return Data, answers the query what happens to the data when a job finishes. There are many places it can go, and you can write modules to send it there.

Chapter 7, Scripting with Runners, shows that SaltStack knows that system administrators have used scripting languages for years, and they have provided a scripting environment that combines Python with the raw power of Salt.

Chapter 8, Adding External File Servers, advises not to just serve files from Salt Master. You can serve files from wherever you want with your own external file server module.

Chapter 9, Connecting to the Cloud, helps you find out how you can update existing cloud modules or add your own. Everyone uses the cloud now, and Salt Cloud connects it to Salt.

Chapter 10, Monitoring with Beacons, helps us to solve the problem that Salt isn't normally associated with monitoring, which is a shame. Beacons are one way to integrate Salt into your monitoring framework.

Chapter 11, Extending the Master, explains that Salt provides a way for you to serve the administrative needs of the Master programmatically. Bonus points for tying in your own authentication system to Salt.

Appendix A, Connecting Different Modules, gives solutions to how to fit the different components even if it is known that Salt modules are designed to play together. This appendix lays out how the different parts connect together.

Appendix B, Contributing Code Upstream, gives you tips to know where the project is screwed up or what features are missing. It doesn't have to be that way with Salt but going back to the community.

What you need for this book

This book assumes a reasonable amount of knowledge of both Salt and the Python programming language. While you may be able to slam out some code without much experience (indeed, that is how the author got started with both), you will find it much easier with these tools already under your belt.

While the examples in this book are tested and functional, they may not be applicable to your needs. They are designed to be simple and easily understood by one who is comfortable with both Python and Salt, while still showcasing a reasonably amount of functionality.

Salt currently has a baseline of Python 2.6, which means that many older Linux distributions are still supported. As of the first edition of this book, Salt does not currently run on the Python 3.x branch. Minion-side examples are expected to work in Windows as well, except when the dependencies that they rely on aren't available.

Because both the Master and the Minion can be run on the same machine, you only need one computer to perform the examples in this book. Many of the examples do refer to software that may not be preinstalled with your operating system. In those cases, the software should still be available for download.

Who this book is for

This book is for both new and existing Salt developers who are looking to build and write new Salt modules. Some prior Python development experience is expected.

Conventions

In this book, you will find a number of text styles that distinguish between different kinds of information. Here are some examples of these styles and an explanation of their meaning.

Code words in text, database table names, folder names, filenames, file extensions, pathnames, dummy URLs, user input, and Twitter handles are shown as follows: "If there is no __virtual__() function, then the module will always be available on every system."

A block of code is set as follows:

```
'''
This module should be saved as salt/modules/mysqltest.py
'''
__virtualname__ = 'mysqltest'


def __virtual__():
    '''
    For now, just return the __virtualname__
    '''
    return __virtualname__


def ping():
    '''
    Returns True

    CLI Example:
        salt '*' mysqltest.ping
    '''
    return True
```

Any command-line input or output is written as follows:

```
#salt-call mymodule.test
```

New terms and **important words** are shown in bold. Words that you see on the screen, for example, in menus or dialog boxes, appear in the text like this: "When you visit your fork on GitHub again, you will see a link that says **New Pull Request**."

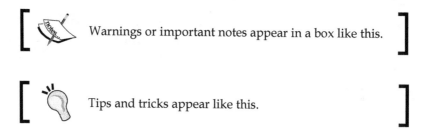

Warnings or important notes appear in a box like this.

Tips and tricks appear like this.

Reader feedback

Feedback from our readers is always welcome. Let us know what you think about this book—what you liked or disliked. Reader feedback is important for us as it helps us develop titles that you will really get the most out of.

To send us general feedback, simply e-mail feedback@packtpub.com, and mention the book's title in the subject of your message.

If there is a topic that you have expertise in and you are interested in either writing or contributing to a book, see our author guide at www.packtpub.com/authors.

Customer support

Now that you are the proud owner of a Packt book, we have a number of things to help you to get the most from your purchase.

Downloading the example code

You can download the example code files for this book from your account at http://www.packtpub.com. If you purchased this book elsewhere, you can visit http://www.packtpub.com/support and register to have the files e-mailed directly to you.

You can download the code files by following these steps:

1. Log in or register to our website using your e-mail address and password.
2. Hover the mouse pointer on the **SUPPORT** tab at the top.
3. Click on **Code Downloads & Errata**.
4. Enter the name of the book in the **Search** box.
5. Select the book for which you're looking to download the code files.
6. Choose from the drop-down menu where you purchased this book from.
7. Click on **Code Download**.

Once the file is downloaded, please make sure that you unzip or extract the folder using the latest version of:

* WinRAR / 7-Zip for Windows
* Zipeg / iZip / UnRarX for Mac
* 7-Zip / PeaZip for Linux

Downloading the color images of this book

We also provide you with a PDF file that has color images of the screenshots/ diagrams used in this book. The color images will help you better understand the changes in the output. You can download this file from `https://www.packtpub. com/sites/default/files/downloads/ExtendingSaltStack_ColorImages.pdf`.

Errata

Although we have taken every care to ensure the accuracy of our content, mistakes do happen. If you find a mistake in one of our books — maybe a mistake in the text or the code — we would be grateful if you could report this to us. By doing so, you can save other readers from frustration and help us improve subsequent versions of this book. If you find any errata, please report them by visiting `http://www.packtpub. com/submit-errata`, selecting your book, clicking on the **Errata Submission Form** link, and entering the details of your errata. Once your errata are verified, your submission will be accepted and the errata will be uploaded to our website or added to any list of existing errata under the Errata section of that title.

To view the previously submitted errata, go to `https://www.packtpub.com/books/ content/support` and enter the name of the book in the search field. The required information will appear under the **Errata** section.

Piracy

Piracy of copyrighted material on the Internet is an ongoing problem across all media. At Packt, we take the protection of our copyright and licenses very seriously. If you come across any illegal copies of our works in any form on the Internet, please provide us with the location address or website name immediately so that we can pursue a remedy.

Please contact us at copyright@packtpub.com with a link to the suspected pirated material.

We appreciate your help in protecting our authors and our ability to bring you valuable content.

Questions

If you have a problem with any aspect of this book, you can contact us at questions@packtpub.com, and we will do our best to address the problem.

Starting with the Basics

1

The vast majority of Salt users see it as a configuration management platform. And in truth, it handles that very well. But it did not start off with that as a design goal. In its early days, Salt was a communication framework that was designed to be useful even to those who did not write code. But for those who were willing, it was also designed to be heavily extensible to those users who had some Python in their toolbelt.

Before we get into writing modules, it will help to have a basic understanding of how the Salt module system works. In this chapter, you'll learn the following:

- How the loader system works
- How Salt uses Python

Using plugins

As Salt was originally designed as a backbone that other software could use to communicate, its earliest purpose was to collect information from a large cluster of both physical and virtual machines, and return that data either to the user or to a database. Various programs, such as `ps`, `du`, and `netstat`, were used to collect that information. Because of that, each program was wrapped with a plugin, which contained various functions to call those programs, and parse the return data.

Those plugins were originally called modules. Later, when other types of module were added to Salt, the original modules began to be referred to as *execution modules*. This is because the execution modules would do the heavy lifting, and other types of module would generally wrap around them and extend their functionality.

Loading modules

Like many data centers, the one that Salt was created in had various servers that used different software packages to perform their work. One server would be running Nginx, while another would be running DNSMasq. It wouldn't make sense to enable the `nginx` module on the DHCP server, or a `dnsmasq` module on the web server. A number of popular programs solve this by allowing the user to configure which plugins will be loaded before starting the service.

Salt had a different way of handling plugins. In a large infrastructure, individual configuration of servers can be costly in terms of time. And as configuration management was added to Salt, a core belief grew that configuration management platforms should require as little configuration themselves as possible. What is the point of using such a suite to save time if so much time is required to get it going in the first place?

This is how the loader system came to be. Salt would always ship with a full set of modules, and Salt would automatically detect modules that would be available, and dynamically load them.

Execution modules are a type of plugin that performs most of the heavy lifting inside of Salt. These were the first to use the loader system, and for a short time there was no other type of module. As the functionality of Salt increased, it quickly became evident that other types of module would be needed. For instance, return output was originally just printed to the console. Then the output was changed to be easier to handle from shell scripts. Then the outputter system was added, so that output could be displayed in JSON, YAML, Python's `pprint`, and any other format that might be useful.

Standard modules

In the beginning, there were some types of module that would always be loaded. The first of these was the `test` module, which required nothing more than Salt's own dependencies; in particular, it would only require Python.

Other modules were also designed for general use, requiring no more than Salt's own dependencies. The `file` module would perform various file-based operations. The `useradd` module would wrap the standard Unix `useradd` program. This was fine, so long as Salt was only used on Unix-like platforms. When users started running Salt on Windows, where those utilities were not readily available, things changed. This is where virtual modules really started to shine.

Virtual modules

Supporting Salt on various platforms, such as both Unix-like and Windows, presents the same problem as whether or not to make the nginx module available: if that platform is installed and available, make the module available. Otherwise, don't. Salt handles the availability problem by implementing virtual modules.

The idea behind a virtual module is that it will contain a piece of code that will detect whether or not its dependencies are met, and if so, the module will be loaded and made available to Salt on that system. We'll get into the details of actually doing this in *Chapter 2, Writing Execution Modules.*

Lazy loading modules

In the beginning, if a module was detected as being loadable, then it would be loaded as the Salt service was started. A number of modules may be loaded for a particular system, which the administrator never intends to use. It may be nice to have them, but in some cases it's better to only load them when they're needed.

When the Salt service starts, the lazy loader will detect which modules may be used on a particular system, but it won't immediately load them into memory. Once a particular module is called, Salt will load it on demand, and then keep it in memory. On a system that typically only uses a small handful of modules, this can result in a much smaller footprint than before.

Extending the loader system

As we said before, the loader system was originally designed for one type of module: what we now call execution modules. Before long, other types of module were added, and that number continues to grow even today.

This book does not include every type of module, but it does cover quite a few. The following list is not comprehensive, but it will tell you much of what is available now, and possibly give you an idea of what other types of module to look at after you finish this book:

- **Execution modules** do much of the heavy lifting inside of Salt. When a program needs to be called, an execution module will be written for it. When other modules need to use that program, they will call out to that module.

- **Grain modules** are used to report information about Minions. **Virtual modules** often rely heavily on these. Configuration can also be defined in grains.

- **Runner modules** were designed to add an element of scripting to Salt. Whereas execution modules run on Minions, a runner module would run on the Master, and call out to the Minions.

- **Returner modules** give Minions a way to return data to something besides the Master, such as a database configured to store log data.

- **State modules** transform Salt from a remote execution framework into a configuration management engine.

- **Renderer modules** allow Salt States to be defined using different file formats, as appropriate.

- **Pillar modules** extend grains, by providing a more centralized system of defining configuration.

- **SDB modules** provide a simple database lookup. They are usually referenced from configuration areas (including grains and pillars) to keep sensitive data from appearing in plaintext.

- **Outputter modules** affect how command-line data output is shown to the user.

- **External file server modules** allow the files that Salt serves to be stored somewhere besides locally on the Master.

- **Cloud modules** are used to manage virtual machines across different compute cloud providers.

- **Beacons** allow various pieces of software, from other Salt components to third-party applications, to report data to Salt.

- **External authentication modules** allow users to access the Master without having to have a local account on it.

- **Wheel modules** provide an API for managing Master-side configuration files.

- **Proxy minion modules** allow devices that cannot run the Salt platform itself to be able to be treated as if they were still full-fledged Minions.

- **Engines** allow Salt to provide internal information and services to long-running external processes. In fact, it may be best to think of engines as programs in their own right, with a special connection to Salt.

- **The Master Tops system** allows States to be targeted without having to use the top.sls file.

- **Roster modules** allow Salt SSH to target Minions without having to use the /etc/salt/roster file.

- **Queue modules** provide a means of organizing function calls.

- The **pkgdb** and **pkgfile modules** allow the Salt Package Manager to store its local database and install Salt formulas into a location outside of the local hard drive.

These modules were generally created as necessity dictated. All of them are written in Python. And while some can be pretty extensive, most are pretty simple to create. In fact, a number of modules that now ship with Salt were actually provided by users who had no previous Python experience.

Loading modules with Python

Python is well suited to building a loader system. Despite being classified as a very high-level language (and not a mid-level language like C), Python has a lot of control over how it manages its own internals. The existence of robust module introspection built into Python was very useful for Salt, as it made the arbitrary loading of virtual modules at runtime a very smooth operation.

Each Salt module can support a function called `__virtual__()`. This is the function that detects whether or not a module will be made available to Salt on that system.

When the `salt-minion` service loads, it will go through each module, looking for a `__virtual__()` function. If none is found, then the module is assumed to have all of its requirements already met, and it can be made available. If that function is found, then it will be used to detect whether the requirements for that module are met.

If a module type uses the lazy loader, then modules that can be loaded will be set aside to be loaded when needed. Modules that do not meet the requirements will be discarded.

Detecting grains

On a Minion, the most important things to load are probably the grains. Although grain modules are important (and are discussed in *Chapter 3*, *Extending Salt Configuration*), there are in fact a number of core grains that are loaded by Salt itself.

A number of these grains describe the hardware on the system. Others describe the operating system that Salt is running on. Grains such as `os` and `os _family` are set, and used later to determine which of the core modules will be loaded.

For example, if the `os_family` grain is set to `redhat`, then the execution module located at `salt/modules/yumpkg.py` will be loaded as the `pkg` module. If the `os_family` grain is set to `debian`, then `salt/modules/aptpkg.py` will be loaded as the `pkg` module.

Using other detection methods

Grains aren't the only mechanism used for determining whether a module should be loaded. Salt also ships with a number of utilities that can be used. The `salt.utils` library contains a number of functions that are often faster than grains, or have more functionality than a simple `name=value` (also known as a key-value pair) configuration can provide.

One example is the `salt.utils.is_windows()` function that, as the name implies, reports whether Salt is being run inside of Windows. If Windows is detected, then `salt/modules/win_file.py` will be loaded as the `file` module. Otherwise, `salt/modules/file.py` will be loaded as the `file` module.

Another very common example is the `salt.utils.which()` function, which reports whether a necessary shell command is available. For instance, this is used by `salt/modules/nginx.py` to detect whether the `nginx` command is available to Salt. If so, then the `nginx` module will be made available.

There are a number of other examples that we could get into, but there is not nearly enough room in this book for all of them. As it is, the most common ones are best demonstrated by example. Starting with *Chapter 2*, *Writing Execution Modules*, we will begin writing Salt modules that make use of the examples that we've already gone over, plus a wealth of others.

Summary

Salt is made possible by the existence of the loader system, which detects which modules are able to load, and then only what is available. Types of module that make use of the lazy loader will only be loaded on demand.

Python is an integral part of Salt, allowing modules to be easily written and maintained. Salt ships with a library of functions that help support the loader system, and the modules that are loaded with it. These files live in various directories under the `salt/` directory in Salt's code base. For example, execution modules live in `salt/modules/`.

This chapter barely brushed the surface of what is possible with Salt, but it got some necessary concepts out of the way. From here on in, the focus will be all about writing and maintaining modules in Python.

2
Writing Execution Modules

Execution modules form the backbone of the workload that Salt performs. They're also easy to write, and the techniques used in writing them form the foundation for writing every other type of Salt module. With a solid understanding of how execution modules work, the functionality of other module types will also be opened up.

In this chapter, we'll talk about:

- The basics of writing Salt modules
- Making use of Salt built-ins
- Using good practices
- Troubleshooting execution modules

Writing Salt modules

There are a few items that are consistent across all Salt modules. These pieces generally work the same way across all module types, though there are a handful of places where you can expect at least a little deviation. We'll cover those in other chapters as we get to them. For now, let's talk about the things that are generally the same.

Hidden objects

It has long been common for programmers to preface functions, variables, and the like with an underscore, if they are only intended to be used internally in the same module. In many languages, objects that are used like this are said to be **private objects**.

Some environments enforce private behavior by not allowing external code to reference those things directly. Other environments allow it, but its use is discouraged. Salt modules fall into the list of environments that enforce private function behavior; if a function inside a Salt module begins with an underscore, it will not even be exposed to other modules that try to call it.

In Python, there is a special type of object whose name begins and ends with two underscores. These "magic methods" are nicknamed **dunder** (meaning double underscore). How Python normally treats them is beyond the scope of this book, but it is important to know that Salt adds some of its own. Some are built-ins, which are generally available in (almost) all module types, whereas others are user-defined objects that Salt will apply special treatment to.

The __virtual__() function

This is a function that can appear in any module. If there is no __virtual__() function, then the module will always be available on every system. If that module is present, then its job is to determine whether the requirements for that module are met. These requirements could be any number of things from configuration settings to package dependencies.

If the requirements are not met, then the __virtual__() function will return `False`. In more recent versions of Salt, it is possible to instead return a tuple containing both the `False` value and a reason why the module cannot be loaded. If they are met, then there are two types of value that it can return. This is where things get just a tad tricky.

Let's say that the module that we are working on is located at `salt/modules/mymodule.py`. If the requirements are met, and the module is to be referred to as `mymodule`, then the __virtual__() function will return `True`. Assuming there is also a function in that module called `test()`, it would be called using the following command:

```
#salt-call mymodule.test
```

If the requirements are met, but this module is to be referred to as `testmodule`, then the __virtual__() function will return the string `testmodule` instead. However, instead of returning that string directly, you should define it before all of the functions using the __virtualname__ variable.

Let's go ahead and start writing a module, using the __virtual__() function and __virtualname__ variable. We won't check for any requirements yet:

```
'''
This module should be saved as salt/modules/mysqltest.py
'''
__virtualname__ = 'mysqltest'


def __virtual__():
    '''
    For now, just return the __virtualname__
    '''
    return __virtualname__


def ping():
    '''
    Returns True

    CLI Example:
        salt '*' mysqltest.ping
    '''
    return True
```

Formatting your code

Before we get any further, I want to point out some important things that you should be aware of now, so that you don't get into any bad habits that need to be fixed later.

The module starts off with a special kind of comment called a docstring. In Salt, this begins and ends with three single quotes, all on one line, by themselves. Do not use double quotes. Do not put text on the same line as the quotes. All public functions must also include a docstring, with the same rules. These docstrings are used internally by Salt, to provide help text to functions such as sys.doc.

 Keep in mind that these guidelines are specific to Salt; Python itself follows a different style. Check *Understanding the Salt style guide* in *Appendix B* for more information.

Take note that the docstring for the ping() function includes a CLI Example. You should always include just enough information to make it clear what the function is meant to do, and at least one (or more, as warranted) command-line examples that demonstrate how to use that function. Private functions do not include a CLI Example.

You should always include two blank lines between any imports and variable declarations at the top and the functions below, and between all functions. There should be no whitespace at the end of the file.

Virtual modules

The primary motivation behind the `__virtual__()` function is not just to rename modules. Using this function allows Salt to not only detect certain pieces of information about the system but also use them to appropriately load specific modules to make certain tasks more generic.

Chapter 1, Starting with the Basics, mentioned some of these examples. `salt/modules/aptpkg.py` contains a number of tests to determine whether it is running on a Debian-like operating system that uses the `apt` suite of tools to perform package management. There are similar tests in `salt/modules/yumpkg.py`, `salt/modules/pacman.py`, `salt/modules/solarispkg.py`, and a number of others. If all of the tests pass for any of those modules, then it will be loaded as the `pkg` module.

If you are building a set of modules like this, it is important to remember that they should all perform as similarly as possible. For instance, all of the `pkg` modules contain a function called `install()`. Every single `install()` function accepts the same arguments, performs the same task (as appropriate for that platform), and then returns data in exactly the same format.

There may be situations where one function is appropriate for one platform, but not another. For example, `salt/modules/aptpkg.py` contains a function called `autoremove()`, which calls out to `apt-get autoremove`. There is no such functionality in `yum`, so that function does not exist in `salt/modules/yumpkg.py`. If there were, then that function would be expected to behave the same way between both files.

Using the salt.utils library

The preceding module will always run, because it doesn't check for requirements on the system. Let's go ahead and add some checking now.

There is an extensive set of tools available to import inside the `salt/utils/` directory. A large number of them live directly under the `salt.utils` namespace, including a very commonly used function called `salt.utils.which()`. When given the name of a command, this function will report the location of that command, if it exists on the system. If it does not exist, then it will return `False`.

Let's go ahead and rework the __virtual__() function to look for a command called mysql:

```
'''
This module should be saved as salt/modules/mysqltest.py
'''
import salt.utils

__virtualname__ = 'mysqltest'


def __virtual__():
    '''
    Check for MySQL
    '''
    if not salt.utils.which('mysql'):
        return False
    return __virtualname__


def ping():
    '''
    Returns True

    CLI Example:
        salt '*' mysqltest.ping
    '''
    return True
```

The salt.utils libraries ship with Salt, but you need to explicitly import them. It is common for Python coders to import only parts of functions. You may find it tempting to use the following import line instead:

```
from salt.utils import which
```

And then use the following line:

```
if which('myprogram'):
```

Although not expressly forbidden in Salt, this is discouraged except when necessary. Although it may require more typing, especially if you use a particular function several times in a particular module, doing so makes it easier to tell at a glance which module a particular function came from.

Cross-calling with the __salt__ dictionary

There are times when it is helpful to be able to call out to another function in another module. For instance, calling external shell commands is a pretty important part of Salt. It's so important in fact that it was standardized in the cmd module. The most common command for issuing shell commands is cmd.run. The following Salt command demonstrates using cmd.run on a Windows Minion:

```
#salt winminon cmd.run 'dir C:\'
```

If you had a need for your execution module to obtain the output from such a command, you would use the following Python:

```
__salt__['cmd.run']('dir C:\')
```

The __salt__ object is a dictionary, which contains references to all of the available functions on that Minion. If a module exists, but its __virtual__() function returns False, then it will not appear in this list. As a function reference, it requires parentheses at the end, with any arguments inside.

Let's go ahead and create a function that tells us whether or not the sshd daemon is running on a Linux system, and listening to a port:

```
def check_mysqld():
    '''
    Check to see if sshd is running and listening

    CLI Example:
        salt '*' testmodule.check_mysqld
    '''
    output = __salt__['cmd.run']('netstat -tulpn | grep mysqld',
python_shell=True)
    if 'tcp' not in output:
        return False
    return True
```

If sshd is running and listening on a port, the output of the netstat -tulpn | grep sshd command should look like this:

```
tcp        0      0 0.0.0.0:3306            0.0.0.0:*
LISTEN      426/mysqld
tcp6       0      0 :::3306                 :::*
LISTEN      426/mysqld
```

If mysqld is running, and listening either on IPv4 or IPv6 (or both), then this function will return True.

This function is far from perfect. There are a number of factors that may cause this command to return a false positive. For instance, let's say you were looking for sshd instead of mysqld. And say you were a fan of American football, and had written your own high-definition football video-streaming service that you called passhd. This may be unlikely, but it's certainly not impossible. And it brings up an important point: when dealing with data received either from users or from computers, **trust but verify**. In fact, you should always assume that somebody is going to try to do something bad, and you should watch for ways to keep them from doing so.

Getting configuration parameters

Whereas some software can be accessed without any special configuration, there is plenty that does require some information to be set up. There are four places that an execution module can get its configuration from: the Minion configuration file, grain data, pillar data, and the master configuration file.

 This is one of those places where Salt built-ins behave differently. Grain and pillar data are available to execution and state modules, but not to other types of module. This is because grain and pillar data is specific to the Minion running the module. Runners, for instance, cannot access this data, because runners are used on the Master; not directly on Minions.

The first place we can look for configuration is from the __opts__ dictionary. When working in modules that execute on a Minion, this dictionary will contain a copy of the data from the Minion configuration file. It may also contain some information that Salt generates on its own during runtime. When accessed from modules that execute on the Master, this data will come from the master configuration file.

It is also possible to set configuration values inside grain or pillar data. This information is accessed using the __grains__ and __pillar__ dictionaries, respectively. The following example shows different configuration values being pulled from each of these locations:

```
username = __opts__['username']
hostname = __grains__['host']
password = __pillar__['password']
```

Since those values may not actually exist, it is better to use Python's dict.get() method, and supply a default:

```
username = __opts__.get('username', 'salt')
hostname = __grains__.get('host', 'localhost')
password = __pillar__.get('password', None)
```

The last place we can store configuration data is inside the master configuration file. All of the Master's configuration can be stored inside a pillar dictionary called `master`. By default, this is not made available to Minions. However, it can be turned on by setting `pillar_opts` to `True` in the `master` configuration file.

Once `pillar_opts` is turned on, you can use commands like this to access a value in the `master` configuration:

```
master_interface = __pillar__['master']['interface']
master_sock_dir = __pillar__.get('master', {}).get('sock_dir',
None)
```

Finally, it is possible to ask Salt to search each of these locations, in turn, for a specific variable. This can be very valuable when you don't care which component carries the information that you need, so long as you can get it from somewhere.

In order to search each of these areas, cross-call to the `config.get()` function:

```
username = __salt__['config.get']('username')
```

This will search for the configuration parameter in the following order:

1. `__opts__` (on the Minion).
2. `__grains__`.
3. `__pillar__`.
4. `__opts__` (on the Master).

Keep in mind that when using `config.get()`, the first value found will be used. If the value that you are looking for is defined in both `__grains__` and `__pillar__`, then the value in `__grains__` will be used.

Another advantage of using `config.get()` is that this function will automatically resolve data that is referred to using `sdb://` URIs. When accessing those dictionaries directly, any `sdb://` URIs will need to be handled manually. Writing and using SDB modules will be covered in *Chapter 3, Extending Salt Configuration*.

Let's go ahead and set up a module that obtains configuration data and uses it to make a connection to a service:

```
'''
This module should be saved as salt/modules/mysqltest.py
'''
import MySQLdb


def version():
```

```
'''
Returns MySQL Version

CLI Example:
    salt '*' mysqltest.version
'''
user = __salt__['config.get']('mysql_user', 'root')
passwd = __salt__['config.get']('mysql_pass', '')
host = __salt__['config.get']('mysql_host', 'localhost')
port = __salt__['config.get']('mysql_port', 3306)
db_ = __salt__['config.get']('mysql_db', 'mysql')
dbc = MySQLdb.connect(
    connection_user=user,
    connection_pass=passwd,
    connection_host=host,
    connection_port=port,
    connection_db=db_,
)
cur = dbc.cursor()
return cur.execute('SELECT VERSION()')
```

This execution module will run on the Minion, but it can connect to any MySQL database using configuration defined in any of the four configuration areas. However, this function is pretty limited. If the MySQLdb driver is not installed, then errors will appear in the Minion's log files when it starts up. If you need to perform other types of query, you will need to grab the configuration values each time. Let's solve each of these problems in turn.

> Did you notice that we used a variable called db_ instead of db? In Python, it is considered better practice to use variable names that are at least three characters long. Salt also considers this to be a requirement. A very common means of accomplishing this for variables that would normally be shorter is to append one or two underscores to the end of the variable name.

Handling imports

A number of Salt modules require third-party Python libraries to be installed. If any of those libraries aren't installed, then the __virtual__() function should return False. But how do you know beforehand whether or not the libraries can be imported?

A very common trick in a Salt module involves attempting to import libraries, and then recording whether or not the import succeeded. This is often accomplished using a variable with a name like HAS_LIBS:

```
try:
    import MySQLdb
    HAS_LIBS = True
except ImportError:
    HAS_LIBS = False


def __virtual__():
    '''
    Check dependencies
    '''
    return HAS_LIBS
```

In this case, Python will attempt to import MySQLdb. If it succeeds, then it will set HAS_LIBS to True. Otherwise, it will set it to False. And because this directly correlates to the value that needs to be returned from the __virtual__() function, we can just return it as it is, so long as we're not changing __virtualname__. If we were, then the function would look like this:

```
def __virtual__():
    '''
    Check dependencies
    '''
    if HAS_LIBS:
        return __virtualname__
    return False
```

Reusing code

There's still the matter of eliminating redundant code between different functions in the same module. In the case of modules that use connection objects (such as a database cursor, or a cloud provider authentication) throughout the code, specific functions are often set aside to gather configuration, and establish a connection.

A very common name for these in-cloud modules is _get_conn(), so let's go with that in our example:

```
def _get_conn():
    '''
    Get a database connection object
    '''
```

```
    user = __salt__['config.get']('mysql_user', 'root')
    passwd = __salt__['config.get']('mysql_pass', '')
    host = __salt__['config.get']('mysql_host', 'localhost')
    port = __salt__['config.get']('mysql_port', 3306)
    db_ = __salt__['config.get']('mysql_db', 'mysql')
    return MySQLdb.connect(
        connection_user=user,
        connection_pass=passwd,
        connection_host=host,
        connection_port=port,
        connection_db=db_,
    )


def version():
    '''
    Returns MySQL Version

    CLI Example:
        salt '*' mysqltest.version
    '''
    dbc = _get_conn()
    cur = dbc.cursor()
    return cur.execute('SELECT VERSION()')
```

This greatly simplifies our code, by turning a large chunk of lines in every function into a single line. Of course, this can be taken quite a bit further. The actual `salt/modules/mysql.py` module that ships with Salt uses a function called `_connect()` instead of `_get_conn()`, and it also has `cur.execute()` abstracted out into its own `_execute()` function. You can see these at Salt's GitHub page:

`https://github.com/saltstack/salt`

Logging messages

Very often, you will perform an operation that requires some kind of message to be logged somewhere. This is especially common when writing new code; it's nice to be able to log debugging information.

Salt has a logging system built in, based on Python's own `logging` library. To turn it on, there are two lines that you'll need to add toward the top of your module:

```
import logging
log = logging.getLogger(__name__)
```

With these in place, you can log messages using a command like this:

```
log.debug('This is a log message')
```

There are five levels of logging that are typically used in Salt:

1. `log.info()`: Information at this level is something that is considered to be important to all users. It doesn't mean anything is wrong, but like all log messages, its output will be sent to STDERR instead of STDOUT (so long as Salt is running in the foreground, and not configured to log elsewhere).

2. `log.warn()`: A message logged from here should indicate to the user that something is not happening as it should be. However, it is not so broken as to stop the code from running.

3. `log.error()`: This denotes that something has gone wrong, and Salt is unable to continue until it is fixed.

4. `log.debug()`: This is not only information that is useful for determining what the program is thinking but is also intended to be useful to regular users of the program for things like troubleshooting.

5. `log.trace()`: This is similar to a debug message, but the information here is more likely to be useful only to developers.

For now, we'll add a `log.trace()` to our `_get_conn()` function, which lets us know when we successfully connect to the database:

```
def _get_conn():
    '''
    Get a database connection object
    '''
    user = __salt__['config.get']('mysql_user', 'root')
    passwd = __salt__['config.get']('mysql_pass', '')
    host = __salt__['config.get']('mysql_host', 'localhost')
    port = __salt__['config.get']('mysql_port', 3306)
    db_ = __salt__['config.get']('mysql_db', 'mysql')
    dbc = MySQLdb.connect(
        connection_user=user,
        connection_pass=passwd,
        connection_host=host,
        connection_port=port,
        connection_db=db_,
    )
    log.trace('Connected to the database')
    return dbc
```

There are certain places where it is tempting to use log messages, but they should be avoided. Specifically, log messages may be used in any function, except for __virtual__(). Log messages used outside of functions, and in the __virtual__() function, make for messy log files that are a pain to read and navigate.

Using the __func_alias__ dictionary

There are a handful of words that are reserved in Python. Unfortunately, some of these words are also very useful for things like function names. For instance, many modules have a function whose job is to list data relevant to that module, and it seems natural to call such a function list(). But that would conflict with Python's list built-in. This poses a problem, since function names are directly exposed to the Salt command.

A workaround is available for this. A __func_alias__ dictionary may be declared at the top of a module, which creates a map between aliases used from the command line and the actual name of the function. For instance:

```
__func_alias__ = {
    'list_': 'list'
}

def list_(type_):
    '''
    List different resources in MySQL
    CLI Examples:
        salt '*' mysqltest.list tables
        salt '*' mysqltest.list databases
    '''
    dbc = _get_conn()
    cur = dbc.cursor()
    return cur.execute('SHOW {0}()'.format(type_))
```

With this in place, the list_ function will be called as mysqltest.list (as in the CLI Example) instead of mysqltest.list_.

Why did we call the variable type_ instead of type? Because type is a Python built-in. But since this function only has one argument, it's not expected that users will need to use type_=<something> as part of their Salt command.

Validating data

From that last piece of code, a number of readers at this point probably have warning bells going off in their heads. It allows for a very common type of security vulnerability called an injection attack. Because the function does not perform any sort of validation on the `type_` variable, it is possible for users to pass in code that can cause destruction, or obtain data that they shouldn't have.

One might think that this isn't necessarily a problem in Salt, because in a number of environments, only trusted users should have access. However, because Salt can be used by a wide range of user types, who may be intended to only have limited access, there are a number of scenarios where an injection attack can be devastating. Imagine a user running the following Salt command:

```
#salt myminion mysqltest.list 'tables; drop table users;'
```

This is often easy to fix, by adding some simple checking to any user input (remember: **trust but verify**):

```
from salt.exceptions import CommandExecutionError


def list_(type_):
    '''
    List different resources in MySQL
    CLI Examples:
        salt '*' mysqltest.list tables
        salt '*' mysqltest.list databases
    '''
    dbc = _get_conn()
    cur = dbc.cursor()
    valid_types = ['tables', 'databases']
    if type_ not in valid_types:
        err_msg = 'A valid type was not specified'
        log.error(err_msg)
        raise CommandExecutionError(err_msg)
    return cur.execute('SHOW {0}()'.format(type_))
```

In this case, we've declared which types are valid before allowing them to be passed in to the SQL query. Even a single bad character will cause Salt to refuse to complete the command. This kind of data validation is often better, because it doesn't try to modify the input data to make it safe to run. Doing so is referred to as *validating user input*.

We've added in another piece of code as well: a Salt exception. There are a number of these available in the `salt.exceptions` library, but `CommandExecutionError` is one that you may find yourself using quite a bit when validating data.

Formatting strings

A quick note on string formatting: Older Python developers may have noticed that we opted to use `str.format()` instead of the older `printf`-style string handling. The following two lines of code do the same thing in Python:

```
'The variable's value is {0}'.format(myvar)
'The variable's value is %s' % myvar
```

String formatting using `str.format()` is just a little faster in Python, and is required in Salt except for in places where it doesn't make sense.

Don't be tempted to use the following shortcut available in Python 2.7.x:

```
'The variable's value is {}'.format(myvar)
```

Because Salt still needs to run on Python 2.6, which doesn't support using {} instead of {0}, this will cause problems for users on older platforms.

The final module

When we put all of the preceding code together, we end up with the following module:

```
'''
This module should be saved as salt/modules/mysqltest.py
'''
import salt.utils

try:
    import MySQLdb
    HAS_LIBS = True
except ImportError:
    HAS_LIBS = False

import logging
log = logging.getLogger(__name__)
```

```
__func_alias__ = {
    'list_': 'list'
}


__virtualname__ = 'mysqltest'


def __virtual__():
    '''
    Check dependencies, using both methods from the chapter
    '''
    if not salt.utils.which('mysql'):
        return False

    if HAS_LIBS:
        return __virtualname__

    return False


def ping():
    '''
    Returns True

    CLI Example:
        salt '*' mysqltest.ping
    '''
    return True


def check_mysqld():
    '''
    Check to see if sshd is running and listening

    CLI Example:
        salt '*' testmodule.check_mysqld
    '''
    output = __salt__['cmd.run']('netstat -tulpn | grep mysqld',
python_shell=True)
    if 'tcp' not in output:
        return False
```

```
        return True


def _get_conn():
    '''
    Get a database connection object
    '''
    user = __salt__['config.get']('mysql_user', 'root')
    passwd = __salt__['config.get']('mysql_pass', '')
    host = __salt__['config.get']('mysql_host', 'localhost')
    port = __salt__['config.get']('mysql_port', 3306)
    db_ = __salt__['config.get']('mysql_db', 'mysql')
    dbc = MySQLdb.connect(
        connection_user=user,
        connection_pass=passwd,
        connection_host=host,
        connection_port=port,
        connection_db=db_,
    )
    log.trace('Connected to the database')
    return dbc


def version():
    '''
    Returns MySQL Version

    CLI Example:
        salt '*' mysqltest.version
    '''
    dbc = _get_conn()
    cur = dbc.cursor()
    return cur.execute('SELECT VERSION()')


def list_(type_):
    '''
    List different resources in MySQL
    CLI Examples:
        salt '*' mysqltest.list tables
        salt '*' mysqltest.list databases
    '''
```

```
dbc = _get_conn()
cur = dbc.cursor()
valid_types = ['tables', 'databases']
if type_ not in valid_types:
    err_msg = 'A valid type was not specified'
    log.error(err_msg)
    raise CommandExecutionError(err_msg)
return cur.execute('SHOW {0}()'.format(type_))
```

Troubleshooting execution modules

As with any programming, the more time you spend writing execution modules, the more likely you are to encounter issues. Let's take a moment to talk about how to troubleshoot and debug your code.

Using salt-call

The salt-call command has always been a valuable tool for testing and troubleshooting code. Without it, you would need to restart the salt-minion service each time you wanted to test new code; believe me, that gets old fast.

Because salt-call doesn't start up a service, it will always run the latest copy of the Salt code. It does do most of the things that the salt-minion service does: it loads grains, connects to the Master (unless told not to) to obtain pillar data, goes through the loader process to decide which modules to load, and then performs the requested command. Pretty much the only thing it doesn't do is keep running.

Using salt-call to issue a command is also the same as using the salt command, except that a target is not required (because the target is the Minion that salt-call is running on):

```
#salt '*' mysqltest.ping
```

```
#salt-call mysqltest.ping
```

You may notice that even though you're issuing salt-call commands on the same machine that will be performing the execution, it tends to run a little slower. There are two reasons for this. First of all, you are still basically starting up the salt-minion service each time, without actually keeping it running. That means that detecting grains, loading modules, and so on will have to happen each time.

To get a feel for how much time this really takes, try comparing execution times both with and without grain detection:

```
# time salt-call test.ping
local:
    True
real    0m3.257s
user    0m0.863s
sys     0m0.197s
# time salt-call --skip-grains test.ping
local:
    True
real    0m0.675s
user    0m0.507s
sys     0m0.080s
```

Of course, if you're testing a module that makes use of grains, this is not an acceptable strategy. The second thing that slows down commands is having to connect to the Master. This doesn't take nearly as much time as grain detection, but it does take a hit:

```
# time salt-call --local test.ping
local:
    True
real    0m2.820s
user    0m0.797s
sys     0m0.120s
```

The `--local` flag doesn't just tell `salt-call` not to talk to the Master. It actually tells `salt-call` to use itself as the Master (meaning, operate in local mode). If your module makes use of pillars or other resources on the Master, then you can just serve them locally instead.

Any configuration in the master configuration file that you need can be copied directly to the `Minion` file. If you're just using the defaults, you don't even need to do that: just copy the necessary files from the Master to the Minion:

```
# scp -r saltmaster:/srv/salt /srv
# scp -r saltmaster:/srv/pillar /srv
```

Once everything is in place, go ahead and fire up `salt-call` with the `--local` flag and get to troubleshooting.

<function> is not available

When I'm writing a new module, one of the first problems I have is getting the module to show up. Quite often this is because of obviously bad code, such as a typo. For instance, if we were to change our import from `salt.utils` to `salt.util`, our module would fail to load:

```
$ grep 'import salt' salt/modules/mysqltest.py
import salt.util
# salt-call --local mysqltest.ping
'mysqltest.ping' is not available.
```

In cases like this, we can find the problem by running `salt-call` in `debug` mode:

```
# salt-call --local -l debug mysqltest.ping
...
[DEBUG   ] Failed to import module mysqltest:
Traceback (most recent call last):
  File "/usr/lib/python2.7/site-packages/salt/loader.py", line 1217, in
_load_module
    ), fn_, fpath, desc)
  File "/usr/lib/python2.7/site-packages/salt/modules/mysqltest.py", line
4, in <module>
    import salt.util
ImportError: No module named util
...
'mysqltest.ping' is not available.
```

Another possibility is that there is a problem with the `__virtual__()` function. This is the one time I would recommend adding log messages to that function:

```
    def __virtual__():
        '''
        Check dependencies, using both methods from the chapter
        '''
        log.debug('Checking for mysql command')
        if not salt.utils.which('mysql'):
            return False

        log.debug('Checking for libs')
        if HAS_LIBS:
            return __virtualname__

        return False
```

However, make sure you pull them out before you ever get into production, or you're going to have some very unhappy users sooner or later.

Downloading the example code

You can download the example code files for this book from your account at http://www.packtpub.com. If you purchased this book elsewhere, you can visit http://www.packtpub.com/support and register to have the files e-mailed directly to you.

You can download the code files by following these steps:

- Log in or register to our website using your e-mail address and password.
- Hover the mouse pointer on the SUPPORT tab at the top.
- Click on Code Downloads & Errata.
- Enter the name of the book in the Search box.
- Select the book for which you're looking to download the code files.
- Choose from the drop-down menu where you purchased this book from.
- Click on Code Download.

Once the file is downloaded, please make sure that you unzip or extract the folder using the latest version of:

- WinRAR/7-Zip for Windows
- Zipeg/iZip/UnRarX for Mac
- 7-Zip/PeaZip for Linux

Summary

Learning how to write execution modules creates an excellent foundation for writing other Salt modules. Salt contains a number of built-ins, many of which are available across all module types. A number of libraries also ship with Salt inside the salt/utils/ directory. And troubleshooting Salt modules is easiest when using the salt-call command, particularly in local mode.

Next up, we'll talk about various types of Salt module that can be used to handle configuration.

Extending Salt Configuration

3

By now you know how to access configuration variables from the various parts of Salt, except for SDB modules, which will be covered in this chapter. But while setting static configuration is all fine and well, it can be very useful to be able to supply that data from an external source. In this chapter, you'll learn about:

- Writing dynamic grains and external pillars
- Troubleshooting grains and pillars
- Writing and using SDB modules
- Troubleshooting SDB modules

Setting grains dynamically

As you already know, grains hold variables that describe certain aspects of a Minion. This could be information about the operating system, the hardware, the network, and so on. It can also contain statically defined user data, which is configured either in /etc/salt/minion or /etc/salt/grains. It is also possible to define grains dynamically using grains modules.

Setting some basic grains

Grains modules are interesting in that so long as the module is loaded, all public functions will be executed. As each function is executed, it will return a dictionary, which contains items to be merged into the Minion's grains.

Let's go ahead and set up a new grains module to demonstrate. We'll prepend the names of the return data with a z so that it is easy to find.

```
'''
Test module for Extending SaltStack

This module should be saved as salt/grains/testdata.py
'''


def testdata():
    '''
    Return some test data
    '''
    return {'ztest1': True}
```

Go ahead and save this file as `salt/grains/testdata.py`, and then use `salt-call` to display all of the grains, including this one:

```
# salt-call --local grains.items
local:
    ----------
...
    virtual:
        physical
    zmqversion:
        4.1.3
    ztest1:
        True
```

Keep in mind that you can also use `grains.item` to display only a single grain:

```
# salt-call --local grains.item ztest
local:
    ----------
    ztest1:
        True
```

It may not look like this module is much good, since this is still just static data that could be defined in the `minion` or `grains` files. But keep in mind that, as with other modules, grains modules can be gated using a `__virtual__()` function. Let's go ahead and set that up, along with a flag of sorts that will determine whether or not this module will load in the first place:

```
import os.path


def __virtual__():
    '''
    Only load these grains if /tmp/ztest exists
    '''
    if os.path.exists('/tmp/ztest'):
        return True
    return False
```

Go ahead and run the following commands to see this in action:

```
# salt-call --local grains.item ztest
local:
    ----------
    ztest:
# touch /tmp/ztest
# salt-call --local grains.item ztest
local:
    ----------
    ztest:
        True
```

This is very useful for gating the return data from an entire module, whether dynamic or, as this module currently is, static.

You may be wondering why that example checked for the existence of a file, rather than checking the existing Minion configuration. This is to illustrate that the detection of certain system properties is likely to dictate how grains are set. If you want to just set a flag inside the `minion` file, you can pull it out of `__opts__`. Let's go ahead and add that to the `__virtual__()` function:

```
def __virtual__():
    '''
    Only load these grains if /tmp/ztest exists
    '''
```

```
if os.path.exists('/tmp/ztest'):
    return True
if __opts__.get('ztest', False):
    return True
return False
```

Go ahead and remove the old flag, and set the new one:

```
# rm /tmp/ztest
# echo 'ztest: True' >> /etc/salt/minion
# salt-call --local grains.item ztest
local:
    ----------
    ztest:
        True
```

Let's go ahead and set up this module to return dynamic data as well. Because YAML is so prevalent in Salt, let's go ahead and set up a function that returns the contents of a YAML file:

```
import yaml
import salt.utils


def yaml_test():
    '''
    Return sample data from /etc/salt/test.yaml
    '''
    with salt.utils.fopen('/etc/salt/yamltest.yaml', 'r') as fh_:
        return yaml.safe_load(fh_)
```

You may notice that we've used `salt.utils.fopen()` instead of a standard Python `open()`. Salt's `fopen()` function wraps Python's `open()` with some extra handling, so that files are closed properly on Minions.

Save your module, and then issue the following commands to see the result:

```
# echo 'yamltest: True' > /etc/salt/yamltest.yaml
# salt-call --local grains.item yamltest
local:
    ----------
    yamltest:
        True
```

(Not) cross-calling execution modules

You may be tempted to try to cross-call an execution module from inside a grains module. Unfortunately, that won't work. The `__virtual__()` function in many execution modules relies heavily on grains. Allowing grains to cross-call to execution modules, before Salt has decided whether or not to even the execution module in the first place, would cause circular dependencies.

Just remember, grains are loaded first, then pillars, then execution modules. If you have code that you plan to use two or more of these types of modules, consider setting up a library for it in the `salt/utils/` directory.

The final grains module

With all of the code we've put together, the resulting module should look like the following:

```
'''
Test module for Extending SaltStack.

This module should be saved as salt/grains/testdata.py
'''
import os.path
import yaml
import salt.utils


def __virtual__():
    '''
    Only load these grains if /tmp/ztest exists
    '''
    if os.path.exists('/tmp/ztest'):
        return True
    if __opts__.get('ztest', False):
        return True
    return False


def testdata():
    '''
    Return some test data
    '''
```

```
        return {'ztest1': True}


    def yaml_test():
        '''
        Return sample data from /etc/salt/test.yaml
        '''
        with salt.utils.fopen('/etc/salt/yamltest.yaml', 'r') as fh_:
            return yaml.safe_load(fh_)
```

Creating external pillars

As you know, pillars are like grains, with a key difference: grains are defined on the Minion, whereas pillars are defined for individual Minions, from the Master.

As far as users are concerned, there's not a whole lot of difference here, except that pillars must be mapped to targets on the Master, using the `top.sls` file in `pillar_roots`. One such mapping might look like this:

```
# cat /srv/pillar/top.sls
base:
  '*':
    - test
```

In this example, we would have a pillar called test defined, which might look like this:

```
# cat /srv/pillar/test.sls
test_pillar: True
```

Dynamic pillars are still mapped in the `top.sls` file, but that's where the similarities end, so far as configuration is concerned.

Configuring external pillars

Unlike dynamic grains, which will run so long as their `__virtual__()` function allows them to do so, pillars must be explicitly enabled in the `master` configuration file. Or, if running in local mode as we will be, in the `minion` configuration file. Let's go ahead and add the following lines to the end of `/etc/salt/minion`:

```
    ext_pillar:
      - test_pillar: True
```

If we were testing this on the Master, we would need to restart the `salt-master` service. However, since we're testing in local mode on the Minion, this will not be required.

Adding an external pillar

We'll also need to create a simple external pillar to get started with. Go ahead and create `salt/pillar/test_pillar.py` with the following content:

```
'''
This is a test external pillar
'''


def ext_pillar(minion_id, pillar, config):
    '''
    Return the pillar data
    '''
    return {'test_pillar': minion_id}
```

Go ahead and save your work, and then test it to make sure it works:

```
# salt-call --local pillar.item test_pillar
local:
    ----------
    test_pillar:
        dufresne
```

Let's go over what's happened here. First off, we have a function called `ext_pillar()`. This function is required in all external pillars. It is also the only function that is required. Any others, whether or not named with a preceding underscore, will be private to this module.

This function will always be passed three pieces of data. The first is the ID of the Minion that is requesting this pillar. You can see this in our example already: the `minion_id` where the earlier example was run was `dufresne`. The second is a copy of the static pillars defined for this Minion. The third is an extra piece of data that was passed to this external pillar in the `master` (or in this case, `minion`) configuration file.

Let's go ahead and update our pillar to show us what each component looks like. Change your ext_pillar() function to look like:

```
def ext_pillar(minion_id, pillar, command):
    '''
    Return the pillar data
    '''
    return {'test_pillar': {
        'minion_id': minion_id,
        'pillar': pillar,
        'config': config,
    }}
```

Save it, and then modify the ext_pillar configuration in your minion (or master) file:

```
ext_pillar:
  - test_pillar: Alas, poor Yorik. I knew him, Horatio.
```

Take a look at your pillar data again:

```
# salt-call --local pillar.item test_pillar
local:
    ----------
    test_pillar:
        ----------
        config:
            Alas, poor Yorik. I knew him, Horatio.
        minion_id:
            dufresne
        pillar:
            ----------
            test_pillar:
                True
```

You can see the test_pillar that we referenced a couple of pages ago. And of course, you can see minion_id, just like before. The important part here is config.

This example was chosen to make it clear where the config argument came from. When an external pillar is added to the ext_pillar list, it is entered as a dictionary, with a single item as its value. The item that is specified can be a string, boolean, integer, or float. It cannot be a dictionary or a list.

This argument is normally used to pass arguments into the pillar from the configuration file. For instance, the `cmd_yaml` pillar that ships with Salt uses it to define a command that is expected to return data in YAML format:

```
ext_pillar:
- cmd_yaml: cat /etc/salt/testyaml.yaml
```

If the only thing that your pillar requires is to be enabled, then you can just set this to True, and then ignore it. However, you must still set it! Salt will expect that data to be there, and you will receive an error like this if it is not:

```
[CRITICAL] The "ext_pillar" option is malformed
```

 Although `minion_id`, `pillar`, and `config` are all passed into the `ext_pillar()` function (in that order), Salt doesn't actually care what you call the variables in your function definition. You could call them Emeril, Mario, and Alton if you wanted (not that you would). But whatever you call them, they must still all be there.

Another external pillar

Let's put together another external pillar, so that it doesn't get confused with our first one. This one's job is to check the status of a web service. First, let's write our pillar code:

```
'''
Get status from HTTP service in JSON format.

This file should be saved as salt/pillar/http_status.py
'''
import salt.utils.http


def ext_pillar(minion_id, pillar, config):
    '''
    Call a web service which returns status in JSON format
    '''
    comps = config.split()
    key = comps[0]
    url = comps[1]
    status = salt.utils.http.query(url, decode=True)
    return {key: status['dict']}
```

You've probably noticed that our docstring states that This file should be saved as salt/pillar/http_status.py. When you check out the Salt codebase, there is a directory called salt/ that contains the actual code. This is the directory that is referred to in the docstring. You will continue to see these comments in the code examples throughout this book.

Save this file as salt/pillar/http_status.py. Then go ahead and update your ext_pillar configuration to point to it. For now, we'll use GitHub's status URL:

```
ext_pillar
  - http_status: github https://status.github.com/api/status.json
```

Go ahead and save the configuration, and then test the pillar:

```
# salt-call --local pillar.item github
local:
    ----------
    github:
        ----------
        last_updated:
            2015-12-02T05:22:16Z
        status:
            good
```

If you need to be able to check the status on multiple services, you can use the same external pillar multiple times, but with different configurations. Try updating your ext_pillar definition to contain two entries:

```
ext_pillar
  - http_status: github https://status.github.com/api/status.json
  - http_status: github2 https://status.github.com/api/status.json
```

Now, this can quickly become a problem. GitHub won't be happy with you if you're constantly hitting their status API. So, as nice as it is to get real-time status updates, you may want to do something to throttle your queries. Let's save the status in a file, and return it from there. We will check the file's timestamp to make sure it doesn't get updated more than once a minute.

Let's go ahead and update the entire external pillar:

```
'''
Get status from HTTP service in JSON format.

This file should be saved as salt/pillar/http_status.py
'''
```

```
import json
import time
import datetime
import os.path
import salt.utils.http


def ext_pillar(minion_id,  # pylint: disable=W0613
               pillar,  # pylint: disable=W0613
               config):
    '''
    Return the pillar data
    '''
    comps = config.split()

    key = comps[0]
    url = comps[1]

    refresh = False
    status_file = '/tmp/status-{0}.json'.format(key)
    if not os.path.exists(status_file):
        refresh = True
    else:
        stamp = os.path.getmtime(status_file)
        now = int(time.mktime(datetime.datetime.now().timetuple()))
        if now - 60 >= stamp:
            refresh = True

    if refresh:
        salt.utils.http.query(url, decode=True, decode_out=status_
file)

    with salt.utils.fopen(status_file, 'r') as fp_:
        return {key: json.load(fp_)}
```

Now we've set a flag called `refresh`, and the URL will only be hit when that flag is
`True`. We've also defined a file that will cache the content obtained from that URL.
The file will contain the name given to the pillar, so it will end up having a name like
`/tmp/status-github.json`. The following two lines will retrieve the last modified
time of the file, and the current time in seconds:

```
stamp = os.path.getmtime(status_file)
now = int(time.mktime(datetime.datetime.now().timetuple()))
```

And comparing the two, we can determine whether the file is more than 60 seconds old. If we wanted to make the pillar even more configurable, we could even move that 60 to the `config` parameter, and pull it from `comps[2]`.

Troubleshooting grains and pillars

While writing grains and pillars, you may encounter some difficulties. Let's take a look at the most common problems you might have.

Dynamic grains not showing up

You may find that when you issue a `grains.items` command from the Master, your dynamic grains aren't showing up. This can be difficult to track down, because grains are evaluated on the Minion, and any errors aren't likely to make it back over the wire to you.

When you find that dynamic grains aren't showing up as you expect, it's usually easiest to log in to the Minion directly to troubleshoot. Open up a shell and try issuing a `salt-call` command to see if any errors manifest themselves. If they don't immediately, try adding `--log-level=debug` to your command to see if any errors have been hiding at that level. Using a `trace` log level might also be necessary.

External pillars not showing up

These can be a little more difficult to pick out. Using `salt-call` is effective in finding errors in grains, because all of the code can be executed without starting up or contacting a service. But pillars come from the Master, unless you're running `salt-call` in `local` mode.

If you are able to install your external pillar code on a Minion for testing, then the steps are the same as for checking for grains errors. But if you find yourself in a situation where the Master's environment cannot be duplicated on a Minion, you will need to use a different tactic.

Stop the `salt-master` service on the Master, and then start it back up in the foreground, with a debug log level:

```
# salt-master --log-level debug
```

Then open up another shell and check the pillars for an affected Minion:

```
# salt <minionid> pillar.items
```

Any errors in the pillar code should manifest themselves in the window with `salt-master` running in the foreground.

Writing SDB modules

SDB is a relatively new type of module, and ripe for development. It stands for Simple Database, and it is designed to allow data to be simple to query, using a very short URI. Underlying configuration can be as complex as necessary, so long as the URI that is used to query it is as simple as possible.

Another design goal of SDB is that URIs can mask sensitive pieces of information from being stored directly inside a configuration file. For instance, passwords are often required for other types of modules, such as the `mysql` modules. But it is a poor practice to store passwords in files that are then stored inside a revision control system such as Git.

Using SDB to look up passwords on the fly allows references to the passwords to be stored, but not the passwords themselves. This makes it much safer to store files that reference sensitive data, inside revision control systems.

There is one supposed function that may be tempting to use SDB for: storing encrypted data on the Minion, which cannot be read by the Master. It is possible to run agents on a Minion that require local authentication, such as typing in a password from the Minion's keyboard, or using a hardware encryption device. SDB modules can be made that make use of these agents, and due to their very nature, the authentication credentials themselves cannot be retrieved by the Master.

The problem is that the Master can access anything that a Minion that subscribes to it can. Although the data may be stored in an encrypted database on the Minion, and although its transfer to the Master is certainly encrypted, once it gets to the Master it can still be read in plaintext.

Getting SDB data

There are only two public functions that are used for SDB: `get` and `set`. And in truth, the only important one of these is `get`, since `set` can usually be done outside of Salt entirely. Let's go ahead and take a look at `get`.

For our example, we'll create a module that reads in a JSON file and then returns the requested key from it. First, let's set up our JSON file:

```
{
    "user": "larry",
    "password": "123pass"
}
```

Go ahead and save that file as /root/mydata.json. Then edit the minion configuration file and add a configuration profile:

```
myjson:
    driver: json
    json_file: /root/mydata.json
```

With those two things in place, we're ready to start writing our module. JSON has a very simple interface, so there won't be much here:

```
'''
SDB module for JSON

This file should be saved as salt/sdb/json.py
'''
from __future__ import absolute_import
import salt.utils
import json


def get(key, profile=None):
    '''
    Get a value from a JSON file
    '''
    with salt.utils.fopen(profile['json_file'], 'r') as fp_:
        json_data = json.load(fp_)
    return json_data.get(key, None)
```

You've probably noticed that we've added a couple of extra things outside of the necessary JSON code. First, we imported something called absolute_import. This is because this file is called json.py, and it's importing another library called json. Without absolute_import, the file would try to import itself, and be unable to find the necessary functions from the actual json library.

The get() function takes two arguments: key and profile. key refers to the key that will be used to access the data that we need. profile is a copy of the profile data that we save in the minion configuration file as myjson.

The SDB URI makes use of these two items. When we build that URI, it will be formatted as:

```
sdb://<profile_name>/<key>
```

For instance, if we were to use the sdb execution module to retrieve the value of key1, our command would look like:

```
# salt-call --local sdb.get sdb://myjson/user
local:
    larry
```

With this module and profile in place, we can now add lines to the minion configuration (or to grains or pillars, or even the master configuration) that look like:

```
username: sdb://myjson/user
password: sdb://myjson/password
```

When a module that uses config.get comes across an SDB URI, it will automatically translate it on the fly to the appropriate data.

Before we move on, let's update this function a little bit to do some error handling. If the user makes a typo in the profile (such as json_fle instead of json_file), or the file being referenced doesn't exist, or the JSON isn't formatted correctly, then this module will start spitting out trace back messages. Let's go ahead and handle all of those, using Salt's own CommandExecutionError:

```
from __future__ import absolute_import
from salt.exceptions import CommandExecutionError
import salt.utils
import json


def get(key, profile=None):
    '''
    Get a value from a JSON file
    '''
    try:
        with salt.utils.fopen(profile['json_file'], 'r') as fp_:
            json_data = json.load(fp_)
        return json_data.get(key, None)
    except IOError as exc:
        raise CommandExecutionError (exc)
    except KeyError as exc:
```

```
        raise CommandExecutionError ('{0} needs to be configured'.
format (exc))
    except ValueError as exc:
        raise CommandExecutionError (
            'There was an error with the JSON data: {0}'.format (exc)
        )
```

IOError will catch problems with a path that doesn't point to a real file. KeyError will catch errors with missing profile configuration (which would happen if one of the items was misspelled). ValueError will catch problems with an improperly formatted JSON file. This will turn errors like:

```
Traceback (most recent call last):
  File "/usr/bin/salt-call", line 11, in <module>
    salt_call()
  File "/usr/lib/python2.7/site-packages/salt/scripts.py", line 333,
in salt_call
    client.run()
  File "/usr/lib/python2.7/site-packages/salt/cli/call.py", line 58,
in run
    caller.run()
  File "/usr/lib/python2.7/site-packages/salt/cli/caller.py", line
133, in run
    ret = self.call()
  File "/usr/lib/python2.7/site-packages/salt/cli/caller.py", line
196, in call
    ret['return'] = func(*args, **kwargs)
  File "/usr/lib/python2.7/site-packages/salt/modules/sdb.py", line
28, in get
    return salt.utils.sdb.sdb_get(uri, __opts__)
  File "/usr/lib/python2.7/site-packages/salt/utils/sdb.py", line 37,
in sdb_get
    return loaded_db[fun](query, profile=profile)
  File "/usr/lib/python2.7/site-packages/salt/sdb/json_sdb.py", line
49, in get
    with salt.utils.fopen(profile['json_fil']) as fp_:
KeyError: 'json_fil'
```

...into errors like this:

```
Error running 'sdb.get': 'json_fil' needs to be configured
```

Setting SDB data

The function that is used for `set` may look strange, because `set` is a Python built-in. That means that the function may not be called `set()`; it must be called something else, and then given an alias using the `__func_alias__` dictionary. Let's go ahead and create a function that does nothing except return the `value` to be set:

```
__func_alias__ = {
    'set_': 'set'
}


def set_(key, value, profile=None):
    '''
    Set a key/value pair in a JSON file
    '''
    return value
```

This will be enough for your purposes with read-only data, but in our case, we're going to modify the JSON file. First, let's look at the arguments that are passed into our function.

You already know that the key points to the data are to be referenced, and that profile contains a copy of the profile data from the Minion configuration file. And you can probably guess that value contains a copy of the data to be applied.

The value doesn't change the actual URI; that will always be the same, no matter whether you're getting or setting data. The execution module itself is what accepts the data to be set, and then sets it. You can see that with:

```
# salt-call --local sdb.set sdb://myjson/password 321pass
local:
    321pass
```

With that in mind, let's go ahead and make our module read in the JSON file, apply the new value, and then write it back out again. For now, we'll skip error handling, to make it easier to read:

```
def set_(key, value, profile=None):
    '''
    Set a key/value pair in a JSON file
    '''
    with salt.utils.fopen(profile['json_file'], 'r') as fp_:
        json_data = json.load(fp_)
```

```
    json_data[key] = value

    with salt.utils.fopen(profile['json_file'], 'w') as fp_:
        json.dump(json_data, fp_)

    return get(key, profile)
```

This function reads in the JSON file as before, then updates the specific value (creating it if necessary), then writes the file back out. When it's finished, it returns the data using the `get()` function, so that the user knows whether it was set properly. If it returns the wrong data, then the user will know that something went wrong. It won't necessarily tell them what went wrong, but it will raise a red flag.

Let's go ahead and add some error handling to help the user know what went wrong. We'll go ahead and add in the error handling from the `get()` function too:

```
def set_(key, value, profile=None):
    '''
    Set a key/value pair in a JSON file
    '''
    try:
        with salt.utils.fopen(profile['json_file'], 'r') as fp_:
            json_data = json.load(fp_)
    except IOError as exc:
        raise CommandExecutionError(exc)
    except KeyError as exc:
        raise CommandExecutionError('{0} needs to be configured'.
format(exc))
    except ValueError as exc:
        raise CommandExecutionError(
            'There was an error with the JSON data: {0}'.format(exc)
        )

    json_data[key] = value

    try:
        with salt.utils.fopen(profile['json_file'], 'w') as fp_:
            json.dump(json_data, fp_)
    except IOError as exc:
        raise CommandExecutionError(exc)

    return get(key, profile)
```

Because we did all of that error handling when reading the file, by the time we get to writing it back again, we already know that the path is value, the JSON is valid, and there are no profile errors. However, there could still be errors in saving the file. Try the following:

```
# chattr +i /root/mydata.json
# salt-call --local sdb.set sdb://myjson/password 456pass
Error running 'sdb.set': [Errno 13] Permission denied: '/root/mydata.
json'
```

We've changed the attribute of the file to make it immutable (read-only), and we can no longer write to the file. Without IOError, we would get an ugly trace back message just like before. Removing the immutable attribute will allow our function to run properly:

```
# chattr -i /root/mydata.json
# salt-call --local sdb.set sdb://myjson/password 456pass
local:
    456pass
```

Using a descriptive docstring

With SDB modules, it is more important than ever to add a docstring that demonstrates how to configure and use the module. Without it, using the module is all but impossible for the user to figure out, and trying to modify a module is even worse.

The docstring doesn't need to be a novel. It should contain enough information to use the module, but not so much that figuring things out becomes confusing and frustrating. You should include not only an example of the profile data but also of an SDB URI to be used with this module:

```
'''
SDB module for JSON

Like all sdb modules, the JSON module requires a configuration profile
to
be configured in either the minion or master configuration file. This
profile
requires very little. In the example:

.. code-block:: yaml
```

```
    myjson:
      driver: json
      json_file: /root/mydata.json
```

The ``driver`` refers to the json module and json_file is the path to the JSON
file that contains the data.

```
.. code-block:: yaml

    password: sdb://myjson/somekey
'''
```

Using more complex configuration

It may be tempting to create SDB modules that make use of more complicated URIs. For instance, it is entirely possible to create a module that supports a URI such as:

```
sdb://mydb/user=curly&group=ops&day=monday
```

With the preceding URI, the key that is passed in would be:

```
user=curly&group=ops&day=monday
```

At that point, it would be up to you to parse out the key and translate it into something usable by your code. However, I strongly discourage it!

The more complex you make an SDB URI, the less it becomes a simple database lookup. You also risk exposing data in an unintended way. Look at the preceding key again. It reveals the following information about the database that holds the information that is supposed to be sensitive:

- There is a field (abstracted or real) that is referred to as user. Since users tend to be lazier than they think, this is likely to point to a real database field called user. If that's true, then this exposes a portion of the database schema.

- There is a group called ops. This means that there are other groups as well. Since *ops* typically refers to a team that performs server operations tasks, does that mean that there's a group called *dev* too? And if the dev group is compromised, what juicy pieces of data do they have for an attacker to steal?

- A day was specified. Does this company rotate passwords on a daily basis? The fact that *monday* was specified implies that there are no more than seven passwords: one for each day of the week.

Rather than putting all of this information into the URL, it is generally better to hide it inside the profile. It's probably safe to assume that `mydb` refers to a database connection (if we called the profile `mysql`, we would be exposing what kind of database connection). Skipping over any database credentials that would be present, we could use a profile that looks like:

```
mydb:
  driver: <some SDB module>
  fields:
    user: sdbkey
    group: ops
    day: monday
```

Assuming that the module in question is able to translate those `fields` into a query, and internally change `sdbkey` to whatever actual `key` was passed in, we could use a URI that looks like:

```
sdb://mydb/curly
```

You can still guess that `curly` refers to a username, which is probably even more obvious when the URI is used with a configuration argument like:

```
username: sdb://mydb/curly
```

However, it doesn't expose the name of the field in the database.

The final SDB module

With all of the code we've put together, the resulting module should look like the following:

```
'''
SDB module for JSON

Like all sdb modules, the JSON module requires a configuration profile to
be configured in either the minion or master configuration file. This profile
requires very little. In the example:

.. code-block:: yaml

    myjson:
      driver: json
      json_file: /root/mydata.json
```

```
The ``driver`` refers to the json module and json_file is the path to
the JSON
file that contains the data.

.. code-block:: yaml

    password: sdb://myjson/somekey
'''
from __future__ import absolute_import
from salt.exceptions import CommandExecutionError
import salt.utils
import json


__func_alias__ = {
    'set_': 'set'
}


def get(key, profile=None):
    '''
    Get a value from a JSON file
    '''
    try:
        with salt.utils.fopen(profile['json_file'], 'r') as fp_:
            json_data = json.load(fp_)
        return json_data.get(key, None)
    except IOError as exc:
        raise CommandExecutionError (exc)
    except KeyError as exc:
        raise CommandExecutionError ('{0} needs to be configured'.
format(exc))
    except ValueError as exc:
        raise CommandExecutionError (
            'There was an error with the JSON data: {0}'.format(exc)
        )


def set_(key, value, profile=None):  # pylint: disable=W0613
    '''
    Set a key/value pair in a JSON file
    '''
    try:
        with salt.utils.fopen(profile['json_file'], 'r') as fp_:
            json_data = json.load(fp_)
```

```
    except IOError as exc:
        raise CommandExecutionError (exc)
    except KeyError as exc:
        raise CommandExecutionError ('{0} needs to be configured'.
format (exc))
    except ValueError as exc:
        raise CommandExecutionError (
            'There was an error with the JSON data: {0}'.format (exc)
        )

    json_data [key] = value

    try:
        with salt.utils.fopen (profile ['json_file'], 'w') as fp_:
            json.dump (json_data, fp_)
    except IOError as exc:
        raise CommandExecutionError (exc)

    return get (key, profile)
```

Using SDB modules

There are a number of places where SDB modules can be used. Because SDB retrieval is built into the `config.get` function in the `config` execution module, the following locations can be used to set a value for a Minion:

- Minion configuration file
- Grains
- Pillars
- Master configuration file

SDB is also supported by Salt Cloud, so you can also set SDB URIs in:

- The main cloud configuration file
- Cloud profiles
- Cloud providers
- Cloud maps

Regardless of where you set an SDB URI, the format is the same:

```
<setting name>: sdb://<profile name>/<key>
```

This can be particularly useful with cloud providers, all of which require credentials, but many of which also use more complex configuration blocks that should be checked into revision control.

Take, for example, the `openstack` Cloud provider:

```
my-openstack-config:
    identity_url: https://keystone.example.com:35357/v2.0/
    compute_region: intermountain
    compute_name: Compute
    tenant: sdb://openstack_creds/tenant
    user: sdb://openstack_creds/username
    ssh_key_name: sdb://openstack_creds/keyname
```

In this organization, `compute_region` and `compute_name` are probably public. And `identity_url` certainly is (else, how would you authenticate?). But the other information should probably be kept hidden.

If you've ever set up OpenStack in Salt Cloud, you've probably used a number of other arguments as well, many of which are probably not sensitive. However, a complex configuration file should probably be kept in a revision control system. With SDB URIs, you can do so without having to worry about exposing the data that is sensitive.

Troubleshooting SDB modules

We've already covered some error handling that can be added to our SDB modules, but you may still encounter problems. Like grains and pillars, the most common involve data not showing up when expected.

SDB data not showing up

You may find that when you include an SDB URI in your configuration, it doesn't resolve as you think it might. If you've made typos in the earlier SDB code, you have probably already figured out that `sdb.get` is more than happy to raise trace backs when there are syntactical errors. But if using `salt-call` on `sdb.get` doesn't raise any errors that you can see, then it may not be a problem in your code.

Before you start to blame other services, it's best to make sure that you're not to blame. Start logging key pieces of information, to make sure it's showing up as you expect. Make sure to add the following lines toward the top of your module:

```
import logging
log = logging.getLogger(__name__)
```

Then you can use `log.debug()` to log those pieces of information. If you're logging sensitive pieces of information, you may want to use `log.trace()` instead, just in case you forget to take the log messages out.

You may want to start with logging the information coming into each function, to make sure it looks like you expect. Let's go ahead and take a look at our `get()` example from earlier, with some logging added in:

```
def get(key, profile=None):
    '''
    Get a value from a JSON file
    '''
    import pprint
    log.debug(key)
    log.debug(pprint.pformat(profile))
    with salt.utils.fopen(profile['json_file'], 'r') as fp_:
        json_data = json.load(fp_)
    return json_data.get(key, None)
```

We've only added a couple of log lines here, but we used Python's `pprint` library to format one of them. The `pprint.pformat()` function formats text that is meant to be stored in a string or passed to a function, instead of just dumping it to STDOUT like `pprint.pprint()` does.

If your SDB module connects to a service, you may discover that the service itself is unavailable. This may be due to unknown or unintended firewall rules, a network error, or actual downtime on the service itself. Scattering log messages throughout your code will help you discover where it is falling down, so that you can address it there.

Summary

The three areas of Salt configuration that can be hooked into using the loader system are dynamic grains, external pillars, and SDB. Grains are generated on the Minion, pillars are generated on the Master, and SDB URIs can be configured in either place.

SDB modules allow configuration to be stored outside, but referenced from, the various parts of the Salt configuration. When accessed from execution modules, they are resolved on the Minion. When accessed from Salt-Cloud, they are resolved on whichever system is running Salt Cloud.

Now that we have configuration out of the way, it's time to dive into configuration management, by wrapping state modules around execution modules.

4
Wrapping States Around Execution Modules

Now that we've covered execution modules and configuration modules, it's time to talk about configuration management. The idea behind a state module is to use execution modules as a mechanism for bringing a resource to a certain state: a package is in an installed state, a service is in a running state, a file's contents match the state defined on the Master. In this chapter, we'll discuss:

- The concepts behind a basic state module layout
- Deciding how far to take each state
- Troubleshooting state modules

Forming a state module

State modules are more structured than most other kinds of modules, but as you'll soon see, that actually makes them easier to write.

Determining state

There is a set of operations that a state module must take in order to perform its job, and as those operations are done, there is certain data that is stored. Let's start off with a pseudo piece of code, and explain each component in turn:

```
def __virtual__():
    '''
    Only load if the necesaary modules available in __salt__
    '''
    if 'module.function' in __salt__:
        return True
```

```
            return False


    def somestate(name):
        '''
        Achieve the desired state

        nane
            The name of the item to achieve statefulness
        '''
        ret = {'name': name,
               'changes': {},
               'result': None,
               'comment': ''}
        if <item is already in the desired state>:
            ret['result'] = True
            ret['comment'] = 'The item is already in the desired state'
            return ret
        if __opts__['test']:
            ret['comment'] = 'The item is not in the desired state'
            return ret
        <attempt to configure the item correctly>
        if <we are able to put the item in the correct state>:
            ret['changes'] = {'desired state': name}
            ret['result'] = True
            ret['comment'] = 'The desired state was successfully achieved'
            return ret
        else:
            ret['result'] = False
            ret['comment'] = 'The desired state failed to be achieved'
            return ret
```

The __virtual__() function

By now, you're already familiar with this function, but I want to mention it here
again. Because execution modules are meant to perform the heavy lifting, it is
crucial to make sure that they are available before trying to make use of them.

There's a good chance you'll need to cross-call multiple functions inside your state
module. Usually, you'll call at least one function to check for the status of the item
in question, and at least one more to bring the item into the desired configuration.
But if they're all in the same execution module, you really only need to check for the
presence of one of them.

Say you were going to write a state that used the `http.query` execution module to perform lookups and make changes to a web resource. That function should always be available, but for the sake of demonstration, we'll assume that we need to check for it. One way to write the function would be:

```
def __virtual__():
    '''
    Check for http.query
    '''
    if 'http.query' in __salt__:
        return True
    return False
```

There is also a shorter way to do this:

```
def __virtual__():
    '''
    Check for http.query
    '''
    return 'http.query' in __salt__
```

Setting up defaults

With the `__virtual__()` function out of the way, we can move on to the stateful function itself. First we set up some default variables in a dictionary. In our example, and in most state modules, the dictionary is called `ret`. This is by convention only, and is not an actual requirement. However, the keys and their data types inside the dictionary are a hard requirement. These keys are:

- name (string) – This is the name of the resource that is passed into the state. This is also known as the ID from the state. For instance, in the following state:

```
nginx:
  - pkg.installed
```

  ○ The name passed in would be `nginx`.

- changes (dictionary) – If the state applies any changes to the Minion, this dictionary will contain an entry for each of the changes that was applied. For instance, if `pkg.installed` was used to install `nginx`, the changes dictionary would look like:

```
{'nginx': {'new': '1.8.0-2', 'old': ''}}
```

  ○ There is no restriction imposed on the type of data stored in changes, so long as changes itself is a dictionary. If changes are made, then this dictionary *must* have something in it.

- result (boolean) – This field is one of three values: True, False, or None. If the specified resource is already in the state that it was meant to be in, or it was successfully made to be in that state, this field will be True. If the resource was not in the correct state, but salt was run with test=True, then this field is set to None. If the resource was not in the correct state, and Salt was unable to put it into the correct state, then this field will be set to False.

  ○ When performing a state run, such as state.highstate, the value of the result will affect the color of the output. States that are True, but have no changes, will be green. States that are True and have changes will be blue. States that are None will be yellow. States that are False will be red.

- comment (string) – This field is entirely freeform: it may contain any comments you want, or no comments. However, it is better to have some comment, even as short as The requested resource is already in the desired state. If the result is None or False, then the comment should contain a message that is as helpful as possible concerning why the resource is not configured properly, and how that may be corrected.

  ○ The defaults that we use in our example will be good for almost any state:

```
ret = {'name': name,
       'changes': {},
       'result': None,
       'comment': ''}
```

Checking for truth

After the defaults have been set, the next task is to check the resource and see whether or not it is in the desired state:

```
if <item is already in the desired state>:
    ret['result'] = True
    ret['comment'] = 'The item is already in the desired state'
    return ret
```

This may be a quick check using a single function in an execution module, or it may consist of much more logic requiring several functions to be cross-called. Don't add any more code here than is necessary to check the state of the resource; remember that all heavy lifting should be performed in the execution module.

If the resource is found to be properly configured, then the result is set to True, a helpful comment is added, and the function returns. If the resource is not properly configured, then we move on to the next section.

Checking for test mode

If the code makes it past the check for truth, then we can assume that something is wrong. But before we make any changes to the system, we need to see whether or not salt was called with test=True.

```
if __opts__['test']:
    ret['comment'] = 'The item is not in the desired state'
    return ret
```

If so, we set a helpful comment for the user, and then return the ret dictionary. If there is any more logic that happens once it has been determined that salt is running in test mode, then it should only be to give the user more helpful information in the comment. No changes should ever be made in test mode!

Attempting to configure the resource

If we get past the check for test mode, then we know that we can try to make changes to correctly configure the resource:

```
<attempt to configure the item correctly>
if <we are able to put the item in the correct state>:
    ret['changes'] = {'desired state': name}
    ret['result'] = True
    ret['comment'] = 'The desired state was successfully achieved'
    return ret
```

Again, this section of the code should only contain enough logic to correctly configure the resource in question, and then notify the user if it was successful. If the change was successful, then we update the changes dictionary, add a comment that describes how those changes were achieved, set the result to True, and then return.

Notifying about False

If we get past that piece of code, we are now assured that something has gone wrong, and that we are unable to fix it:

```
else:
    ret['result'] = False
    ret['comment'] = 'The desired state failed to be achieved'
    return ret
```

This is the most important section of code to be helpful to the user, because user interaction will likely be required to fix whatever the problem is.

It could be that the SLS file was just poorly written, and that the next state run will fix it. It could also be that the state module has a bug that needs to be fixed. Or there could be some other situation that is beyond Salt's ability to control, such as a web service that is temporarily unavailable. The comment should contain as much information as is helpful to track down and fix the problem, and no more. This is also the time to set the result to `False` before `returning`.

Example: checking an HTTP service

There is already a state for contacting web services: the `http.query` state. However, it is very general-purpose, and using it directly has limited use. In fact, it doesn't really have the logic to do much more than check whether a URL responds as expected. In order to make it more intelligent, we need to add some logic on our own.

Checking credentials

Let's start by setting up our `docstring`, a library import, and a `__virtual__()` function with some credentials for a theoretical web service:

```
'''
This state connects to an imaginary web service.
The following credentials must be configured:

    webapi_username: <your username>
    webapi_password: <your password>

This module should be saved as salt/states/fake_webapi.py
'''
import salt.utils.http


def __virtual__():
    '''
    Make sure there are credentials
    '''
    username = __salt__['config.get']('webapi_username', False)
    password = __salt__['config.get']('webapi_password', False)
    if username and password:
        return True
    return False
```

In this case, we aren't checking for the existence of the `http.query` function; as we said before, it's already there. But this module won't function without being able to connect to the web service, so we do a quick check to make sure the credentials are in place.

We aren't checking to see if the service itself responds, or if the credentials are correct. The `__virtual__()` function is checked when the Minion starts, and doing all that checking then is unnecessary and, in the event of downtime, possibly inaccurate. It will also slow the Minion from loading. It is better to do that checking later, when we actually make the call to the service.

The first stateful function

Next, we need to set up a state function. For our example, we're going to allow users to make sure that a specific user's account on that web service is locked out. First, we set up our defaults, and then check to see if that user's account has been locked out yet:

```python
def locked(name):
    '''
    Ensure that the user is locked out
    '''
    username = __salt__['config.get']('webapi_username', False)
    password = __salt__['config.get']('webapi_password', False)

    ret = {'name': name,
           'changes': {},
           'result': None,
           'comment': ''}

    result = salt.utils.http.query(
        'https://api.example.com/v1/users/{0}'.format(name),
        username=username,
        password=password,
        decode=True,
        decode_type='json',
    )

    if result('dict', {}).get('access', '') == 'locked':
        ret['result'] = True
        ret['comment'] = 'The account is already locked'
        return ret
```

You may see a problem right away. Making an authenticated web call is a little heavy, especially when you have to decode the return data, no matter how you do it. We're going to make another web call in this function, and then more in other functions. Let's break out what we can into another function:

```
def _query(action, resource='', data=None):
    '''
    Make a query against the API
    '''
    username = __salt__['config.get']('webapi_username', False)
    password = __salt__['config.get']('webapi_password', False)

    result = salt.utils.http.query(
        'https://api.example.com/v1/{0}/{1}'.format(action, resource),
        username=username,
        password=password,
        decode=True,
        decode_type='json',
        data=data,
    )


def locked(name):
    '''
    Ensure that the user is locked out
    '''
    ret = {'name': name,
           'changes': {},
           'result': None,
           'comment': ''}

    result = _query('users', name)
    if result('dict', {}).get('access', '') == 'locked':
        ret['result'] = True
        ret['comment'] = 'The account is already locked'
        return ret
```

The new _query() function expects at least one argument: the type of query (action) that is going to be performed against the API. It's very common for this kind of API to be expected to list all items for that query if a specific resource isn't specified, so we've allowed the resource to be blank. We've also set up another optional parameter called data, which we'll make use of in a moment.

Now we have a check for whether the account is locked, and are able to `return` `True` if it is. If we get past that point, we know the account isn't locked, so let's do our check for `test` mode:

```
if __opts__['test']:
    ret['comment'] = 'The {0} account is not locked'.format(name)
    return ret
```

This part is easy enough; we have all of the information that is needed for `test` mode, and we don't need to do anything else besides `return` it. Let's go ahead and try to apply the correct setting to the account.

```
_query('users', name, {'access': 'locked'})
```

Remember that `data` option? We used it to pass in a dictionary that sets the access value for that user to `locked`. This is also a very common way to modify data with a web API.

Of course, we don't necessarily know that the setting was applied correctly, so let's do one more check, just to make sure:

```
    result = _query('users', name)
    if result('dict', {}).get('access', '') == 'locked':
        ret['changes'] = {'locked': name}
        ret['result'] = True
        ret['comment'] = 'The {0} user account is now locked'.
format(name)
        return ret
    else:
        ret['result'] = False
        ret['comment'] = 'Failed to set the {0} user account to
locked'.format(name)
        return ret
```

If the account is now locked, then we can return that we were successful. If the account is still not locked, then we can return a failure message.

Another stateful function

Let's go ahead and add another function, to allow a user account to be unlocked. We'll also take this opportunity to show you the entire module, with all of the public and private functions:

```
'''
This state connects to an imaginary web service.
The following credentials must be configured:
```

```
        webapi_username: <your username>
        webapi_password: <your password>

This module should be saved as salt/states/fake_webapi.py
'''
import salt.utils.http


def __virtual__():
    '''
    Make sure there are credentials
    '''
    username = __salt__['config.get']('webapi_username', False)
    password = __salt__['config.get']('webapi_password', False)
    if username and password:
        return True
    return False


def _query(action, resource='', data=None):
    '''
    Make a query against the API
    '''
    username = __salt__['config.get']('webapi_username', False)
    password = __salt__['config.get']('webapi_password', False)

    result = salt.utils.http.query(
        'https://api.example.com/v1/{0}/{1}'.format(action, resource),
        username=username,
        password=password,
        decode=True,
        decode_type='json',
        data=data,
    )
return result


def locked(name):
    '''
    Ensure that the user is locked out
    '''
    ret = {'name': name,
           'changes': {},
           'result': None,
```

```
                    'comment': ''}

        result = _query('users', name)
        if result('dict', {}).get('access', '') == 'locked':
            ret['result'] = True
            ret['comment'] = 'The account is already locked'
            return ret

        if __opts__['test']:
            ret['comment'] = 'The {0} account is not locked'.format(name)
            return ret

        _query('users', name, {'access': 'locked'})

        result = _query('users', name)
        if result('dict', {}).get('access', '') == 'locked':
            ret['changes'] = {'locked': name}
            ret['result'] = True
            ret['comment'] = 'The {0} user account is now locked'.
format(name)
            return ret
        else:
            ret['result'] = False
            ret['comment'] = 'Failed to set the {0} user account to
locked'.format(name)
            return ret


def unlocked(name):
    '''
    Ensure that the user is NOT locked out
    '''
    ret = {'name': name,
           'changes': {},
           'result': None,
           'comment': ''}

    result = _query('users', name)
    if result('dict', {}).get('access', '') == 'unlocked':
        ret['result'] = True
        ret['comment'] = 'The account is already unlocked'
        return ret

    if __opts__['test']:
```

```
        ret['comment'] = 'The {0} account is locked'.format(name)
        return ret


    _query('users', name, {'access': 'unlocked'})

    result = _query('users', name)
    if result('dict', {}).get('access', '') == 'unlocked':
        ret['changes'] = {'locked': name}
        ret['result'] = True
        ret['comment'] = 'The {0} user account is no longer locked'.
format(name)
        return ret
    else:
        ret['result'] = False
        ret['comment'] = 'Failed to unlock the {0} user account'.
format(name)
        return ret
```

You can see that there's not much difference between these two functions. In fact, really, they do exactly the same thing, but with opposing logic: one locks an account and one unlocks an account.

It is very common for a state module to contain two opposites for the same configuration. You will frequently see function names like `installed` and `removed`, `present` and `absent`, and `running` and `dead`.

Troubleshooting state modules

Even though the code is more structured, it can be a little tricky to troubleshoot state modules. This is because you need to test all four types of return results:

- True – The resource is already correctly configured
- None – The resource is not correctly configured, and `test` mode is True
- True with changes – The resource was not correctly configured, but now it is
- False – The resource could not be correctly configured

What makes this even trickier is that in the course of troubleshooting, you are likely to change configuration to be correct, and then incorrect, and then back again several times before the code is right. I suggest breaking it up.

Step 1: test for truth

Your first step, after setting up your defaults, is to check whether the resource is correctly configured. This is likely to require you to manually toggle settings to make sure it is properly checking both desired and undesired configuration. Add two returns: one for `True` and one for `False`:

```
ret = {'name': name,
       'changes': {},
       'result': None,
       'comment': ''}
if <item is already in the desired state>:
    ret['result'] = True
    ret['comment'] = 'The item is already in the desired state'
    return ret
ret['result'] = False
return ret
```

You can remove those last two lines later, once you know the code is correct. You don't need to set up an entire SLS file to test your state; you can use `state.single` to perform a one-off state command:

```
# salt-run --local state.single fake_webapi.locked larry
```

Step 2: test mode

Once you're sure it's correctly detecting the current configuration, manually set the configuration to an undesired value, and make sure `test` mode is working properly:

Step 3: applying changes

When you are sure that your code will not try to apply changes without first checking for test mode, you can move on to applying changes.

This is the trickiest part, for two reasons. First, you'll end up setting and resetting your configuration a lot. This can be tedious at best, but there's no avoiding it. Second, you'll be both setting the correct configuration, and then testing to see if it was set, at the same time:

```
<attempt to configure the item correctly>
if <we are able to put the item in the correct state>:
    ret['changes'] = {'desired state': name}
    ret['result'] = True
    ret['comment'] = 'The desired state was successfully achieved'
    return ret
```

```
else:
    ret['result'] = False
    ret['comment'] = 'The desired state failed to be achieved'
    return ret
```

You may think that you can split this part up, but before long you're likely to realize that in order to make sure the configuration was applied properly, you still need to perform the same check as you would normally be performing in your own tests, so you might as well get it out of the way now.

Testing opposites

Thankfully, if you're writing functions that perform opposite functions, the second one tends to go much faster. That's because once you have the first one out of the way, you can keep running it to reset the configuration back to the undesired value for the second one. In the case of our example, once you are able to lock an account, you can easily lock it while testing the unlock functionality.

Summary

State modules are more structured than execution modules, but that often makes them easier to write. A state's return result can be True (green), None (yellow), True with changes (blue), or False (red). State modules frequently contain pairs of functions that perform opposing functionality.

Now that you know how to write state modules, it's time to take a look at the data that we pass to them. Next up: renderers!

5
Rendering Data

Having the ability to write your own execution and state modules is powerful from a developer's point of view, but you cannot overlook being able to provide that kind of power to users who do not have the ability to provide modules of their own.

Renderers allow users to provide data to various parts of Salt using different kinds of data input formats. The handful of renderers that ship with Salt cover the majority of use cases, but what if your users need to apply data in a specialized format? Or even a more common one that is not yet supported, such as XML? In this chapter, we'll discuss:

- Writing renderers
- Troubleshooting renderers

Understanding file formats

By default, Salt uses YAML for its various files. There are two primary reasons for this:

- YAML is easily converted into Python data structures
- YAML is easy for humans to read and modify

Salt configuration files must be in YAML as well (or JSON, which can be read by YAML parsers), but other files such as states, pillars, reactors, and so on can use other formats. A data serialization format is the most common, but any format that can be translated into a Python dictionary will do just fine.

For example, there are three different Python renderers that ship with Salt: `py`, `pyobjects`, and `pydsl`. Each has its strengths and weaknesses, but the end result is the same: they execute Python code that results in a dictionary, which is then passed into Salt.

Generally speaking, you will find two types of renderers inside of Salt. The first returns data in a Python data structure. Both serializers and code-based modules fit into this category. The second is for managing text formatting and templating. Let's talk about each in turn, and then build our own renderers later on in the chapter.

Serializing data

Data can be stored in any number of formats, but in the end, that data must be something that can be turned into instructions. Formats such as YAML and JSON are obvious choices, because they are easy to modify and mirror the resulting data structures in the program that uses them. Binary formats such as Message Pack aren't as easily modified by humans, but they still result in the same data structures.

Other formats, such as XML, are more difficult because they don't directly resemble the internal data structures of programs like Salt. They're great for modeling code that makes heavy use of classes, but Salt doesn't make much use of such code. However, when you know how such a format can be converted into a data structure that Salt can use, then building a renderer for it is not difficult.

Working with templates

Templates are important because they allow end users to use certain programmatic elements without having to write actual modules. Variables are certainly one of the most critical elements of a templating engine, but other constructs such as loops and branching can also give a lot of power to the user.

Templating renderers differ from data-serializing renderers in that instead of returning data in a dictionary format, which is then ingested by Salt, they return data that must be converted at least one more time, using a data-serialization renderer.

This may seem counterintuitive on some levels, but the use of render pipes brings these two elements together.

Using render pipes

Render pipes are based on Unix pipes; data can be passed from module to module through a series of pipes, in order to arrive at the final data structure. You may not realize it, but if you've ever written an SLS file, you've used a render pipe.

To set up a render pipe, you add a line to the top of the file to be rendered, which contains the classic Unix hashbang, followed by the renderers to be used, in the order to be used, separated by the pipe character. The default rendering sequence is effectively:

```
#!jinja|yaml
```

This means that the file in question will be first parsed by Jinja2, and compiled into a format that can be read by the YAML library.

It's generally not reasonable or necessary to pipe more than two different renderers together; the more that are used, the more complicated the resulting file is to understand by humans, and the greater the chance for errors. Generally, a templating engine that adds programmatic shortcuts, and a data serializer, is plenty. One notable exception is the `gpg` renderer, which can be used for encryption-at-rest scenarios. The hashbang for this would look like:

```
#!jinja|yaml|gpg
```

Building a serializing renderer

Renderers are reasonably easy to build, because they typically do little more than import a library, shove data through it, and then return the result. Our example renderer will make use of Python's own Pickle format.

The basic structure

Outside of any necessary imports, a renderer requires only a `render()` function. The most important argument is the first. As with other modules, the name of this argument is not important to Salt, so long as it is defined. Because our example uses the `pickle` library, we'll use `pickle_data` as our argument name.

Other arguments are also passed into renderers, but in our case we'll only use them for troubleshooting. In particular, we need to accept `saltenv` and `sls`, with the defaults shown later. We'll cover those in the *Troubleshooting Renderers* section, but for now we'll just use `kwargs` to cover them.

We also need to start with a special kind of `import`, called `absolute_import`, that allows us to import the `pickle` library from a file that's also called `pickle`.

Let's go ahead and lay out the module, and then talk about the components in the render() function:

```
'''
Render Pickle files.

This file should be saved as salt/renderers/pickle.py
'''
from __future__ import absolute_import
import pickle
from salt.ext.six import string_types


def render(pickle_data, saltenv='base', sls='', **kwargs):
    '''
    Accepts a pickle, and renders said data back to a python dict.
    '''
    if not isinstance(pickle_data, string_types):
        pickle_data = pickle_data.read()

    if pickle_data.startswith('#!'):
        pickle_data = pickle_data[(pickle_data.find('\n') + 1):]
    if not pickle_data.strip():
        return {}
    return pickle.loads(pickle_data)
```

This function does not do much, other than:

- First, check to see whether the data being passed in is a string, and if not, treat it as a file-like object.
- Check for the existence of a #!, indicating the use of an explicit render pipe. Because that pipe is handled elsewhere, and it will cause errors with the pickle library, discard it.
- Check to see whether the resulting content is empty. If so, return an empty dictionary.
- Run the data through the pickle library, and return the result.

If you start comparing this code with the renderers that ship with Salt, you'll find that many of them are almost identical. This is in part because so many data serialization libraries in Python use exactly the same methods.

Let's put together a file that can be used. The example data that we'll use is:

```
apache:
  pkg:
    - installed
    - refresh: True
```

The best way to create this file is with Python itself. Go ahead and open up a Python shell and type the following commands:

```
>>> import pickle
>>> data = {'apache': {'pkg': ['installed', {'refresh': True}]}}
>>> out = open('/srv/salt/pickle.sls', 'w')
>>> pickle.dump(data, out)
>>> out.close()
```

When you exit out of the Python shell, you should be able to open this file in your favorite text editor. When you add a hashbang line to the top that specifies the `pickle` renderer, your file will probably look like this:

```
#!pickle
(dp0
S'apache'
p1
(dp2
S'pkg'
p3
(lp4
S'installed'
p5
a(dp6
S'refresh'
p7
I01
sass.
```

Save the file, and use `salt-call` to test out your renderer. This time, we'll tell Salt to dump out the resulting SLS, as Salt sees it:

```
# salt-call --local state.show_sls pickle --out=yaml
local:
  apache:
    __env__: base
```

```
__sls__: !!python/unicode pickle
pkg:
- installed
- refresh: true
- order: 10000
```

Salt's state compiler adds some extra information that it uses internally, but we can see that the basics of what we requested are there.

Building a templating renderer

Building a renderer that handles templating files is not that different from one that does serialization. In fact, the renderer itself is pretty much the same, outside of the library-specific code. This time, we'll use a Python library called `tenjin`. You may need to install it using pip:

```
# pip install tenjin
```

Templating with Tenjin

This module makes use of a third-party library, so there will be a `__virtual__()` function to make sure it's installed:

```
'''
Conver a file using the Tenjin templating engine

This file should be saved as salt/renderers/tenjin.py
'''
from __future__ import absolute_import
try:
    import tenjin
    from tenjin.helpers import *
    HAS_LIBS = True
except ImportError:
    HAS_LIBS = False
from salt.ext.six import string_types


def __virtual__():
    '''
    Only load if Tenjin is installed
    '''
```

```
        return HAS_LIBS


def render(tenjin_data, saltenv='base', sls='', **kwargs):
    '''
    Accepts a tenjin, and renders said data back to a python dict.
    '''
    if not isinstance(tenjin_data, string_types):
        tenjin_data = tenjin_data.read()

    if tenjin_data.startswith('#!'):
        tenjin_data = tenjin_data[(tenjin_data.find('\n') + 1):]
    if not tenjin_data.strip():
        return {}

    template = tenjin.Template(input=tenjin_data)
    return template.render(kwargs)
```

The `render()` function itself is fundamentally identical to the one that we used for `pickle`, except for the last two lines, which handles the templating engine slightly differently.

Take note of the `kwargs` that are passed into this function. Templating engines generally have the ability to merge in an external data structure, which can be used with the various data structures in the templating engine itself. Salt will make some data available inside kwargs, so we'll pass that in for Tenjin to use.

Using a templating renderer

Of course, you'll need a hashbang line in your SLS files as before, but since our Tenjin renderer isn't set up to return straight data, you will need to add the name of the desired data-serialization renderer to your render pipe. We'll use the same actual SLS data as before, but with a couple of Tenjin-specific elements added:

```
#!tenjin|yaml
<?py pkg = 'apache'?>
<?py refresh = True?>
#{pkg}:
  pkg:
    - installed
    - refresh: #{refresh}
```

We haven't done anything special here, just set a couple of variables, and then used them. The resulting content will be in YAML format, so we've added `yaml` to our render pipe.

A number of templating engines, including Tenjin, have the ability to process templates that output either strings (as we've done in our example), or an actual data structure, such as what a data serializer would return. When using such a library, take a moment to consider how much of it you plan to use, and whether it makes sense to create two distinct renderers for it: one for data and one for strings.

Testing is much the same as before:

```
# salt-call --local state.show_sls tenjin --out yaml
local:
  apache:
    pkg:
    - installed
    - refresh: true
    - order: 10000
    __sls__: !!python/unicode tenjin
    __env__: base
```

We can see slight differences between our first example and our second, but those differences just show which module was used to render the data.

Troubleshooting renderers

Because renderers are so often used to manage SLS files, it is often easiest to troubleshoot them using the state compiler, as we have been doing already in this chapter.

First, generate a small SLS file that contains the specific elements which you need to test. This will either be a data file in the format that a serialization engine uses, or a text-based file that results in a data-serialization file format. If you are writing a templating renderer, it is often easiest to just use YAML.

The `state` execution module contains a number of functions that exist primarily for troubleshooting. We used `state.show_sls` in our examples, with `--out yaml`, because it displays the output in a format that we're already used to in our SLS files. However, some other useful functions are:

- `state.show_low_sls`: Shows data from a single SLS file, after it has been converted to low data by the State compiler. Low data is often easier to visualize when writing state modules.

- `state.show_highstate`: Shows all of the states, as they would be applied to a Minion, according to the `top.sls` file. The output from this will look as if all of the SLS files have been shoved together. This can be useful when troubleshooting rendering issues that you believe span across multiple SLS files.

- `state.show_lowstate`: The data returned from this function is the same as what `state.show_highstate` returns, but after being processed by the state compiler. Again, this is like a long version of `state.show_low_sls`.

Summary

Renderers are used to convert various file formats into a data structure that is usable internally by Salt. Data-serialization renderers return data in a dictionary format, whereas templating renderers return data that can be processed by a data serializer. Both types of renderer look the same, and require a `render()` function.

Now that we know how to handle the data going into Salt, it's time to look at the data coming back out of Salt. Next up: handling return data.

6
Handling Return Data

When the Salt Master issues a command to a Minion and the task completes successfully, there will always be return data. The `salt` command normally listens for return data, and if it is sent back in time, it will be displayed using an outputter. But whether or not that happens, the Minion will always send return data back to the Master, and any other destinations configured as returners.

This chapter is all about handling that return data, using both returner and outputter modules. We'll talk about:

- How data is returned to the Master
- Writing returner modules
- Extending returners to be used as external job caches
- Troubleshooting returners
- Writing outputter modules
- Troubleshooting outputters

Returning data to external destinations

The most important type of module to handle return data is called a returner. When the Master publishes a task (called a job) to a target, it assigns a job ID (or JID) to it. When a Minion finishes that job, it sends the resulting data back to the Master, along with the JID that is associated with it.

Returning data to the master

Salt's architecture is based on the publish-subscribe pattern, known colloquially as pub/sub. In this design, one or more clients subscribe to a message queue. When a message is published to the queue, any current subscribers receive a copy, which they usually process in some way.

Salt in fact makes use of two message queues, both of which are managed by the Master. The first is used by the Master to publish commands to its Minions. Each Minion can see the messages published to this queue, but they will only react to them if the Minions are included in the target. A message targeted to `'*'` will be processed by all Minions that are connected, whereas one targeted to `192.168.0.0/16` using the `-s` command-line option will only be processed by Minions whose IP address starts with `192.168`.

The second message queue is also hosted by the Master, but messages are published to it from Minions, and the Master itself is the subscriber. These messages are normally stored in the Master's job cache. Returners can be configured to send these messages to other destinations, and some returners can also use those destinations as the job cache itself. If the `salt` command is still listening when those messages are received, then it will also send the data to an outputter.

Listening to event data

Every time a message is published to the queue, an event is also fired along Salt's event bus. You can use the `state.event` runner to listen to the event bus and display those messages in real time.

Make sure you have the `salt-master` service running, and the `salt-minion` service on at least one machine connected to it. On the Master, run the following command:

```
# salt-run state.event
```

In another terminal, issue a command to one or more Minions:

```
# salt '*' test.ping
```

In the terminal that is running the event listener, you will see the job go out to the Minions:

```
Event fired at Sun Dec 20 12:04:15 2015
*************************
Tag: 20151220120415357444
Data:
{'_stamp': '2015-12-20T19:04:15.387417',
 'minions': ['trotter',
             'achatz']}
```

The information contained in this event is no more than a timestamp indicating when the job was created, and a list of Minions that the specified target (in our example, all of them) are expected to execute the job and return data from it.

This is a very small task, so almost immediately you should start seeing return data show up from Minions. Because each Minion responds individually, you will see one entry per Minion:

```
Event fired at Sun Dec 20 12:04:15 2015
*************************
Tag: salt/job/20151220120415357444/ret/dufresne
Data:
{'_stamp': '2015-12-20T19:04:15.618340',
 'cmd': '_return',
 'fun': 'test.ping',
 'fun_args': [],
 'id': 'dufresne',
 'jid': '20151220120415357444',
 'retcode': 0,
 'return': True,
 'success': True}
```

Take note of the tags used for each event. The event that was created when the Master created the job has a tag that contains just the JID. Each return event contains a tag that is namespaced with salt/job/<JID>/ret/<Minion ID>.

After a few seconds, the salt command will also return, and notify you which Minions did and did not finish the job that was assigned to them:

```
# salt '*' test.ping
achatz:
    True
trotter:
    Minion did not return. [Not connected]
```

In our case, achatz was active, and able to return True as requested. Unfortunately, trotter isn't around anymore, and so wasn't able to do what we need.

When returners listen to Minions

Each time the Master receives a response from a Minion, it will call out to a returner. If a job targets, say, 400 Minions, then you should expect the returner to be executed 400 times, one for each Minion.

This is not normally a problem. If a returner connects to a database, then that database is likely to be able to handle 400 responses very quickly. However, if you create a returner that sends messages to humans, such as the SMTP returner that ships with Salt, then you can expect 400 individual e-mails to be sent; one per Minion.

There is one more thing to keep in mind: returners were originally designed to be executed on Minions. The idea behind this was to offload the work to Minions so that in a large environment, a Master wouldn't be required to handle all of the work necessary to, say, connect to a database once per Minion per job.

Returners can now be run either by a Master or by a Minion, and when writing your own returners, you should expect either to be a possibility. We will discuss the configuration for this later in the chapter, when we talk about job caches.

Let's go ahead and see an example of this in action. Connect to one of your Minions and stop the `salt-minion` service. Then start it running in the foreground, using the `info` log level:

```
# salt-minion --log-level info
```

Then connect to the Master and issue a job directly to it:

```
# salt dufresne test.ping
dufresne:
    True
```

Switch back to the Minion, and you will see some information about the job:

```
[INFO    ] User sudo_techhat Executing command test.ping with jid
2015122012464707029
[INFO    ] Starting a new job with PID 25016
[INFO    ] Returning information for job: 2015122012464707029
```

Now issue the command again, but with the `--return` flag set to `local`. This returner will display the return data directly to the local console:

```
# salt dufresne --return local test.ping
dufresne:
    True
```

Switch back to the Minion again to check out the return data:

```
[INFO    ] User sudo_techhat Executing command test.ping with jid
20151220124658909637
[INFO    ] Starting a new job with PID 25066
[INFO    ] Returning information for job: 20151220124658909637
{'fun_args': [], 'jid': '20151220124658909637', 'return': True,
'retcode': 0, 'success': True, 'fun': 'test.ping', 'id': 'dufresne'}
```

Your first returner

Go ahead and open up `salt/returners/local.py`. There's not much in here, but what we're interested in is the `returner()` function. It's very, very small:

```
def returner(ret):
    '''
    Print the return data to the terminal to verify functionality
    '''
    print(ret)
```

In fact, all it does is accept return data as `ret`, and then print it to the console. It doesn't even attempt any sort of pretty printing; it just dumps it as is.

This is in fact the bare minimum that a returner needs: a `returner()` function that accepts a dictionary, and then does something with it. Let's go ahead and create our own returner, which stores job information locally in JSON format.

```
'''
Store return data locally in JSON format

This file should be saved as salt/returners/local_json.py
'''
import json
import salt.utils


def returner(ret):
    '''
    Open new file, and save return data to it in JSON format
    '''
    path = '/tmp/salt-{0}-{1}.json'.format(ret['jid'], ret['id'])
    with salt.utils.fopen(path, 'w') as fp_:
        json.dump(ret, fp_)
```

Save this file, on a Minion, and then issue a job to it. It doesn't matter whether or not you restart the `salt-minion` service; returner modules use `LazyLoader`. But we'll go ahead and use `salt-call` anyway:

```
# salt-call --local --return local_json test.ping
local:
    True
```

Go ahead and look inside the `/tmp/` directory:

```
# ls -l /tmp/salt*
-rw-r--r-- 1 root   root   132 Dec 20 13:03 salt-20151220130309936721-
dufresne.json
```

If you take a look inside that file, you will see return data that looks very similar to what we received from the local returner, except that it is in JSON format:

```
# cat /tmp/salt-20151220130309936721-dufresne.json
{"fun_args": [], "jid": "20151220130309936721", "return": true,
"retcode": 0, "success": true, "fun": "test.ping", "id": "dufresne"}
```

Using job caches

In a way, our JSON returner is a job cache, because it caches return data. Unfortunately, it doesn't contain any code to do anything with the data once it's saved. By updating the logic and adding a few functions, we can extend the functionality.

Right now, our returner behaves like little more than a set of log files. Let's change it to behave more like a flat-file database. We'll use the JID as the access key, and format the directory structure based on the dates in the JIDs:

```
import json
import os.path
import salt.utils
import salt.syspaths


def _job_path(jid):
    '''
    Return the path for the requested JID
    '''
    return os.path.join(
        salt.syspaths.CACHE_DIR,
        'master',
```

```
            'json_cache',
            jid[:4],
            jid[4:6],
            jid[6:],
        )


def returner(ret):
    '''
    Open new file, and save return data to it in JSON format
    '''
    path = os.path.join(_job_path(ret['jid']), ret['id']) + '/'
    __salt__['file.makedirs'](path)
    ret_file = os.path.join(path, 'return.json')
    with salt.utils.fopen(ret_file, 'w') as fp_:
        json.dump(ret, fp_)
```

We haven't changed anything except for the directory structure, and how it's handled. The private function _job_path() will standardize the directory structure, and can be used by future functions. We've also made use of salt.syspaths to detect where Salt is configured to keep cache files on this machine. When run against a Minion called dufresne, the path used to store the return data will look like:

```
/var/cache/salt/master/json_cache/2015/12/21134608721496/dufresne/
return.json
```

We'll also need to store information about the job itself. The return.json file contains some information about the job, but not all of it.

Let's go ahead and add a function that saves the metadata about the job. This metadata is called the load, and contains a jid, a dictionary called clear_load that contains the bulk of the metadata, and a list called minions, which will contain a list of all of the Minions that were included in the target:

```
def save_load(jid, clear_load, minions=None):
    '''
    Save the load to the specified JID
    '''
    path = os.path.join(_job_path(jid)) + '/'
    __salt__['file.makedirs'](path)

    load_file = os.path.join(path, 'load.json')
    with salt.utils.fopen(load_file, 'w') as fp_:
        json.dump(clear_load, fp_)
```

```
if 'tgt' in clear_load:
    if minions is None:
        ckminions = salt.utils.minions.CkMinions(__opts__)
        # Retrieve the minions list
        minions = ckminions.check_minions(
                clear_load['tgt'],
                clear_load.get('tgt_type', 'glob')
                )
    minions_file = os.path.join(path, 'minions.json')
    with salt.utils.fopen(minions_file, 'w') as fp_:
        json.dump(minions, fp_)
```

Once again, we generate the path that the data will be written to. The `clear_load` dictionary will be written to `load.json` inside that path. The list of Minions is a little trickier, since it may contain an empty list. If it does, we use a class inside `salt.utils.minions` called `CkMinions` to generate that list, based on the target that was used for the job. Once we have that list, we write it as `minions.json`.

Testing this is also a little trickier, because it requires a job that was generated from the Master in order to generate all of the metadata that is needed. We also need to let the Master know that we're using an external job cache.

First, edit the master configuration file and add an `ext_job_cache` line, which is set to `local_json`:

```
ext_job_cache: local_json
```

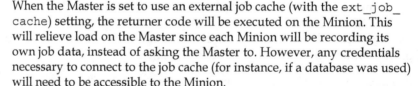

External job cache versus Master job cache

When the Master is set to use an external job cache (with the `ext_job_cache`) setting, the returner code will be executed on the Minion. This will relieve load on the Master since each Minion will be recording its own job data, instead of asking the Master to. However, any credentials necessary to connect to the job cache (for instance, if a database was used) will need to be accessible to the Minion.

When the Master is set to use a Master job cache (with the `master_job_cache`) setting, the returner code will be executed on the Master. This will increase the workload on the Master, but will save you from having to make credentials available to Minions.

Once you've turned on the job cache, let's go ahead and restart both the Master and the Minion, and try things out:

```
# systemctl restart salt-master
# systemctl restart salt-minion
# salt dufresne test.ping
dufresne:
    True
# find /var/cache/salt/master/json_cache/
/var/cache/salt/master/json_cache/2015/12/
/var/cache/salt/master/json_cache/2015/12/21184312454127
/var/cache/salt/master/json_cache/2015/12/21184312454127/load.json
/var/cache/salt/master/json_cache/2015/12/21184312454127/dufresne
/var/cache/salt/master/json_cache/2015/12/21184312454127/dufresne/return.json
/var/cache/salt/master/json_cache/2015/12/21184312454127/minions.json
# cat /var/cache/salt/master/json_cache/2015/12/21184312454127/load.json
{"tgt_type": "glob", "jid": "20151221184312454127", "cmd": "publish",
"tgt": "dufresne", "kwargs": {"delimiter": ":", "show_timeout": true,
"show_jid": false}, "ret": "local_json", "user": "sudo_larry", "arg": [],
"fun": "test.ping"}
# cat /var/cache/salt/master/json_cache/2015/12/21184312454127/minions.json
["dufresne"]
```

Now we have the information being saved, but we don't have any way to retrieve it, outside of manually looking inside the files. Let's go ahead and complete our returner with some functions that can read the data.

First, we need a function that just returns information about the job load:

```
    def get_load(jid):
        '''
        Return the load data for a specified JID
        '''
        path = os.path.join(_job_path(jid), 'load.json')
        with salt.utils.fopen(path, 'r') as fp_:
            return json.load(fp_)
```

We also need a function that gets the return data from each job. These two functions will be used together by the jobs runner:

```python
def get_jid(jid):
    '''
    Return the information returned when the specified JID was
executed
    '''
    minions_path = os.path.join(_job_path(jid), 'minions.json')
    with salt.utils.fopen(minions_path, 'r') as fp_:
        minions = json.load(fp_)

    ret = {}
    for minion in minions:
        data_path = os.path.join(_job_path(jid), minion, 'return.
json')
        with salt.utils.fopen(data_path, 'r') as fp_:
            ret[minion] = json.load(fp_)

    return ret
```

We don't need to restart the Master to be able to test this, since the jobs runner doesn't require the Master to be running:

```
# salt-run jobs.print_job 20151221184312454127
20151221184312454127:
    ----------
    Arguments:
    Function:
        test.ping
    Result:
        ----------
        dufresne:
            ----------
            fun:
                test.ping
            fun_args:
            id:
                dufresne
            jid:
                20151221184312454127
```

```
            retcode:
                0
            return:
                True
            success:
                True
    StartTime:
        2015, Dec 21 18:43:12.454127
    Target:
        dufresne
    Target-type:
        glob
    User:
        sudo_techhat
```

We'll also need a function that returns a list of JIDs, along with some basic information about their associated jobs. This function will make use of another import, which we will use to quickly locate the load.json files:

```
import salt.utils.find


def get_jids():
    '''
    Return a dict mapping all JIDs to job information
    '''
    path = os.path.join(
        salt.syspaths.CACHE_DIR,
        'master',
        'json_cache'
    )

    ret = {}
    finder = salt.utils.find.Finder({'name': 'load.json'})
    for file_ in finder.find(path):
        with salt.utils.fopen(file_) as fp_:
            data = json.load(fp_)
        if 'jid' in data:
            ret[data['jid']] = {
                'Arguments': data['arg'],
                'Function': data['fun'],
```

```
                    'StartTime': salt.utils.jid.jid_to_time(data['jid']),
                    'Target': data['tgt'],
                    'Target-type': data['tgt_type'],
                    'User': data['user'],
                }

        return ret
```

Once again, we test this with the `jobs` runner:

```
# salt-run jobs.list_jobs
20151221184312454127:
    ----------
    Arguments:
    Function:
        test.ping
    StartTime:
        2015, Dec 21 18:43:12.454127
    Target:
        dufresne
    Target-type:
        glob
    User:
        sudo_techhat
```

The final module

Once we have compiled all of the code together, the final module will look like this:

```
'''
Store return data locally in JSON format

This file should be saved as salt/returners/local_json.py
'''
import json
import os.path
import salt.utils
import salt.utils.find
import salt.utils.jid
```

```
import salt.syspaths


def _job_path(jid):
    '''
    Return the path for the requested JID
    '''
    return os.path.join(
        salt.syspaths.CACHE_DIR,
        'master',
        'json_cache',
        jid[:4],
        jid[4:6],
        jid[6:],
    )


def returner(ret):
    '''
    Open new file, and save return data to it in JSON format
    '''
    path = os.path.join(_job_path(ret['jid']), ret['id']) + '/'
    __salt__['file.makedirs'](path)
    ret_file = os.path.join(path, 'return.json')
    with salt.utils.fopen(ret_file, 'w') as fp_:
        json.dump(ret, fp_)


def save_load(jid, clear_load, minions=None):
    '''
    Save the load to the specified JID
    '''
    path = os.path.join(_job_path(jid)) + '/'
    __salt__['file.makedirs'](path)

    load_file = os.path.join(path, 'load.json')
    with salt.utils.fopen(load_file, 'w') as fp_:
        json.dump(clear_load, fp_)
            minions = ckminions.check_minions(
                    clear_load['tgt'],
                    clear_load.get('tgt_type', 'glob')
                    )
        minions_file = os.path.join(path, 'minions.json')
```

```
        with salt.utils.fopen(minions_file, 'w') as fp_:
            json.dump(minions, fp_)


def get_load(jid):
    '''
    Return the load data for a specified JID
    '''
    path = os.path.join(_job_path(jid), 'load.json')
    with salt.utils.fopen(path, 'r') as fp_:
        return json.load(fp_)


def get_jid(jid):
    '''
    Return the information returned when the specified JID was
executed
    '''
    minions_path = os.path.join(_job_path(jid), 'minions.json')
    with salt.utils.fopen(minions_path, 'r') as fp_:
        minions = json.load(fp_)

    ret = {}
    for minion in minions:
        data_path = os.path.join(_job_path(jid), minion, 'return.
json')
        with salt.utils.fopen(data_path, 'r') as fp_:
            ret[minion] = json.load(fp_)

    return ret


def get_jids():
    '''
    Return a dict mapping all JIDs to job information
    '''
    path = os.path.join(
        salt.syspaths.CACHE_DIR,
        'master',
        'json_cache'
    )

    ret = {}
    finder = salt.utils.find.Finder({'name': 'load.json'})
```

```
for file_ in finder.find(path):
    with salt.utils.fopen(file_) as fp_:
        data = json.load(fp_)
    if 'jid' in data:
        ret[data['jid']] = {
            'Arguments': data['arg'],
            'Function': data['fun'],
            'StartTime': salt.utils.jid.jid_to_time(data['jid']),
            'Target': data['tgt'],
            'Target-type': data['tgt_type'],
            'User': data['user'],
        }

return ret
```

Troubleshooting returners

As you have seen, there are a number of different pieces of Salt that use different parts of the returner. Some of these require a Master to be running, which makes them a little trickier to troubleshoot. Here are some strategies that can help.

Testing with salt-call

The returner() function can be tested with the salt-call command. When doing this, simple print statements can be used to display information to your console. If there are typos, Python will display error messages. If the problem pertains to technically valid, but still buggy code, then print statements can be used to track down the problem.

Testing with the Master running

The save_load() function requires a job to be generated on the Master, to one or more Minions. This of course requires both a Master and at least one Minion to be running. You can run them in the foreground in separate terminals, in order to see the output from print statements:

```
# salt-master --log-level debug
# salt-minion --log-level debug
```

If you are using ext_job_cache, then it is the Minion that you will want to be watching. If you are using the master_job_cache, then watch the Master.

Testing with runners

The `get_load()`, `get_jid()`, and `get_jids()` functions are all used by the `jobs` runner. This runner doesn't require either Master or Minions to be running; it only requires that the data store that is being used by the returner is available. Again, `print` statements inside these functions will display information when the `jobs` runner is used.

Writing outputter modules

When the `salt` command is used, any return data that is received during the wait period will be displayed to the user. Outputter modules are used in this case to display that data to the console (or more accurately, to STDOUT), usually in a format that is somewhat user-friendly.

Pickling our output

Because Salt already ships with a `json` outputter, we'll take advantage of the fact that output data is technically going to STDOUT, and put together an `outputter` that uses a serializer (`pickle`) that may dump binary data:

```
'''
Pickle outputter

This file should be saved as salt/output/pickle.py
'''
from __future__ import absolute_import
import pickle


def output(data):
    '''
    Dump out data in pickle format
    '''
    return pickle.dumps(data)
```

This `outputter` is about as simple as it gets. The only required function is called `output()`, and it accepts a dictionary. It doesn't matter what the dictionary is called, so long as the function has one defined.

The `pickle` library is built into Python, and as you saw with the `pickle` renderer, is very easy to use: we just tell it to dump out the data into a string, which is returned to Salt.

As usual, we can test this `outputter` using `salt-call`:

```
# salt-call --local test.ping --out pickle
(dp0
S'local'
p1
I01
s.
```

If you take a look at some of the other outputters that ship with Salt, you'll notice that some are just as simple. Even the `json` outputter doesn't do any extra work, outside of formatting the output. Most execution modules will make use of the `nested` outputter by default. `nested` uses a format based on YAML, but with color-coded data. The `state` functions, however, use the `highstate` outputter, which builds upon nested to return an aggregated version of the data, with statistics about the success of the state run.

Troubleshooting outputters

Outputters can be one of the easiest types of module to troubleshoot. You should be able to test any of them using the `salt-call` command.

When testing, start with a simple `test.ping`, just to make sure that you are getting some output in the first place. Once you're satisfied that your `output()` function is returning simple data that looks correct, take a look at `grains.items`, which will make use of both lists and dictionaries.

You may find it useful to test your output against another outputter that is known to work well. I find that the `pprint` outputter tends to be the most succinct at displaying data in a format that is easy to read, but takes the least amount of screen real-estate:

```
# salt-call --local grains.items --out pickle
# salt-call --local grains.items --out pprint
```

Summary

Return data command is always sent to the Master, even after the `salt` command has finished listening for it. The event bus picks up those messages and can store them in an external job cache. If the `salt` command is still listening, then it will be displayed using an `outputter`. But specifying a returner will always send return data someplace to be processed, so long as the Master itself is still running.

Returners can be specified using the `--return` flag, or can be set to run by default on the Minion using the `ext_job_cache master` configuration option, or on the Master using the `master_job_cache master` configuration option.

Now that we have ways of handling return data, it's time to create more intelligent processes to execute our commands. Next up: runners.

Scripting with Runners

One of the design principles behind Unix is that programs should be small, doing only one thing, but doing it well. Execution modules follow this pattern, using functions that normally do only one thing, grouped with related functions into modules. When a function is executed, it performs that job, and then returns.

In Unix, these small programs can be combined together using a shell script, which ties them into a more powerful tool. Salt's runner system brings that element of scripting to Salt, using the same language that Salt itself is written in: Python. In this chapter, we will discuss:

- Connecting to Salt's local client
- Adding extra logic to execution modules
- Troubleshooting runners

Using Salt's local client

Runners were originally designed to run on the Master, to combine multiple jobs across Minions into one complete task. In order to communicate with those Minions, a runner needs to use `local_client`. Unlike other components, this is not built directly into runners; you need to initialize the client yourself. Let's set up a quick example:

```
import salt.client
client = salt.client.get_local_client(__opts__['conf_file'])
minions = client.cmd('*', 'test.ping', timeout=__opts__['timeout'])
```

These three lines form the basis of setting up and using the local client. First, we import the `salt.client` library. Then, we instantiate a client object, which is used to communicate to Salt. When creating that client object, you do need to tell it where to find Salt's configuration file. Luckily, this is something we get for free in the `__opts__` dictionary, and we're unlikely to need to change it, so that line in your code will probably always look exactly like what we've done here.

The last line uses the `client` object to issue a command to a target. What is returned from that is a list of the Minions that responded, within the specified timeout. Let's go ahead and break out that last line into components, and discuss each one:

```python
minions = client.cmd(
    '*',  # The target to use
    'test.ping',  # The command to issue
    timeout=__opts__['timeout']  # How long to wait for a response
)
```

By now, you should be used to using `'*'` as a target, and know that it refers to all of the Minions. And you should know that `test.ping` is a standard command, often used to check and see which Minions are responding. The timeout is also required, but there's rarely a need to use anything but the configured timeout, so `__opts__['timeout']` will almost always be sufficient.

Scripting with the local client

Runners, like other Salt modules, are based around functions inside of modules. The preceding code is technically correct, but it's not where it needs to be in order to be used as a runner. Let's go ahead and create a runner module called `scan`, which we'll use to collect various pieces of information about all of our Minions:

```python
'''
Scan Minions for various pieces of information

This file should be saved as salt/runners/scan.py
'''
import salt.client


__func_alias__ = {
    'up_': 'up'
}

def up_():
    '''
    Return a list of minions which are responding
```

```
    ''''
    client = salt.client.get_local_client(__opts__['conf_file'])
    minions = client.cmd('*', 'test.ping', timeout=__opts__
['timeout'])
    return sorted(minions.keys())
```

At the moment, we don't have much, but it is functional as a runner. Our first function is called up, but since it's considered bad form to use function names shorter than three characters, we've defined it as up_(), and used __func_alias__ to make it callable as up.

This function will connect to the local client, issue a test.ping to all Minions, and then return a list of which Minions responded. If we were to return minions instead of minions.keys(), then we would get a list of all of the Minions that responded, and what they responded with. Since we know that test.ping will always return True (assuming that it returns in the first place), we can skip returning that data. We also sorted the list of Minions, to make it easier to read.

To execute this function, use the salt-run command:

```
# salt-run scan.up
- achatz
- dufresne
```

Why not create the client connection at the top of the module, so that every function can have access to it? Due to the way the loader presents modules to Salt, the __opts__ dictionary is only available inside functions, so we can't use it at the top of the module. You could hardcode the correct path, but as we all know, hardcoded data is also poor form, and to be avoided.

If you only want to define the client once, then consider using a private function called _get_conn(), which returns the connection object. However, since it would only contain one line of code, and that line is unlikely to ever change, it's probably not worth it.

The scan.up function that we've created tells us which Minions are responding, but you may be more interested in which ones aren't responding. Those are more likely to tell you when Minions are having connection issues. Let's go ahead and add a function called down():

```
import salt.key


def down():
```

```
'''
Return a list of minions which are NOT responding
'''
minions = up_()
key = salt.key.Key(__opts__)
keys = key.list_keys()
return sorted(set(keys['minions']) - set(minions))
```

First, we need to know which Minions have responded, but we already have a function that reports that to us, so we just use the response from that.

We also need a list of the Minions that are expected to return. We can get this by creating a `salt.key` object, and asking it for a list of Minions whose keys have been accepted by the Master.

Now that we have a list of which Minions should respond, we remove the Minions that did respond from that list, and if any Minions are left in the list, then they are the ones that we can assume are down. As before, we've sorted the list of Minions as we return them, to make it easy to read:

```
# salt-run scan.down
- adria
- trotter
```

Using different targets

One major difference that separates the `salt-run` command from the `salt` command is the inability to specify a target on the command line. This is because runners are designed to be able to determine their targets on their own.

Let's go ahead and update the `up_()` and `down()` functions to allow the user not only to specify their own target but also a target type:

```
def up_(tgt='*', tgt_type='glob'):
    '''
    Return a list of minions which are responding
    '''
    client = salt.client.get_local_client(__opts__['conf_file'])
    minions = client.cmd(
        tgt,
        'test.ping',
        expr_form=tgt_type,
        timeout=__opts__['timeout']
    )
```

```
    return sorted(minions.keys())


def down(tgt='*', tgt_type='glob'):
    '''
    Return a list of minions which are NOT responding
    '''
    minions = up_(tgt, tgt_type)

    key = salt.key.Key(__opts__)
    keys = key.list_keys()

    return sorted(set(keys['minions']) - set(minions))
```

In our function, the `tgt` argument refers to the target. The local client requires a target to be specified anyway, so we just replace `'*'` in our function with `tgt`. The `tgt_type` is the type of target to be used. By default, Salt uses a target type of `glob` anyway, but users can specify something else (`pcre`, `list`, and so on) if they need to. The name of this argument in the local client is `expr_form`. Check the "Target Selection Options" in the output of `salt --help` to see which options are supported in your version of Salt.

Combining jobs to add more logic

One of the most powerful things about runners is the ability to take the output from one job, and use it to start another job. First, let's define a few things about our infrastructure:

- We're using Salt Virt to manage some VMs.
- Some Minions run hypervisors; others are VMs that run inside those hypervisors. Some do not run a hypervisor, but are also not a VM.
- A number of different operating systems are being used, such as Suse, CentOS, and Ubuntu.

With that in mind, we need to run a report of which hypervisors are running on which operating systems.

We could use this Salt command to discover which Minions are running which operating systems:

```
# salt '*' grains.item os
```

And we could run this command to find out which Minions are virtualized:

```
# salt '*' grains.item virtual
```

But just because a Minion's `virtual` grain is set to `physical` doesn't mean it's a hypervisor. We could run this command to find out which Minions are running hypervisors:

```
# salt '*' virt.is_hyper
```

However, there's nothing that can aggregate those data together and tell us which hypervisors are running which operating systems; so let's put together a function that can do that:

```python
def hyper_os():
    '''
    Return a list of which operating system each hypervisor is running
    '''
    client = salt.client.get_local_client(__opts__['conf_file'])
    minions = client.cmd(
        '*',
        'virt.is_hyper',
        timeout=__opts__['timeout']
    )

    hypers = []
    for minion in minions:
        if minions[minion] is True:
            hypers.append(minion)

    return client.cmd(
        hypers,
        'grains.item',
        arg=('os',),
        expr_form='list',
        timeout=__opts__['timeout']
    )
```

After we create our `client` object, our first job is to see which Minions actually have a hypervisor running. Then we loop through that list and save the ones that are in another list called `hypers`. Because we're storing that in list form, we can pass it to the client again with an `expr_form` of `list`.

We've also added something new. The `grains.item` function expects a single argument that tells it which grain to look up. When you need to pass a list of unnamed arguments to a function, pass it in as `arg`. When we run this runner, our output will look something like this:

```
# salt-run scan.hyper_os
dufresne:
    ----------
    os:
        Arch
```

Let's say we want to be able to run an arbitrary Salt command on any machine that shows up in that hypervisor list. We're going to do two things in our next bit of code. We're going to break `hyper_os()` into two functions, called `hypers()` and `hyper_os()`, and then add a new function called `hyper_cmd()`, which will make use of the `hypers()` function:

```python
def hypers(client=None):
    '''
    Return a list of Minions that are running hypervisors
    '''
    if client is None:
        client = salt.client.get_local_client(__opts__['conf_file'])

    minions = client.cmd(
        '*',
        'virt.is_hyper',
        timeout=__opts__['timeout']
    )

    hypers = []
    for minion in minions:
        if minions[minion] is True:
            hypers.append(minion)

    return hypers


def hyper_os():
    '''
```

```
    Return a list of which operating system each hypervisor is running
    '''
    client = salt.client.get_local_client(__opts__['conf_file'])

    return client.cmd(
        hypers(client),
        'grains.item',
        arg=('os',),
        expr_form='list',
        timeout=__opts__['timeout']
    )


def hyper_cmd(cmd, arg=None, kwarg=None):
    '''
    Execute an arbitrary command on Minions which run hypervisors
    '''
    client = salt.client.get_local_client(__opts__['conf_file'])

    if arg is None:
        arg = []

    if not isinstance(arg, list):
        arg = [arg]

    if kwarg is None:
        kwarg = {}

    return client.cmd(
        hypers(client),
        cmd,
        arg=arg,
        kwarg=kwarg,
        expr_form='list',
        timeout=__opts__['timeout']
    )
```

You may notice that each function is able to create its own `client` object, including `hypers()`. This allows us to use `scan.hypers` on its own. However, it also allows us to pass in a `client` object from other functions. This can save a lot of time over creating one `client` object per Salt command.

The `hyper_cmd()` function allows us to pass in arguments in a number of different ways, or none at all if necessary. Using it without any arguments would look like this:

```
# salt-run scan.hyper_cmd test.ping
```

Using it with an unnamed argument would look like:

```
# salt-run scan.hyper_cmd test.ping
```

It starts to get tricky when you pass in a list of arguments. By default, Salt is able to convert YAML that is passed in on the command line into data structures that can be used inside of Salt. This means that you can run this command:

```
# salt-run scan.hyper_cmd test.arg [one,two]
```

And Salt will automatically translate [one,two] into a list containing a string of one followed by a string of two. However, that is not what will happen if you run this command:

```
# salt-run scan.hyper_cmd test.arg one,two
```

In this case, Salt will think that you have passed in a string whose value is one,two. If you wanted to allow users to enter lists like that, you would need to detect and parse them out manually.

It gets even trickier if you want to pass in named arguments. The following is valid:

```
salt-run scan.hyper_cmd network.interface kwarg="{'iface':'wlp3s0'}"
```

But it's pretty horrible to ask users to type that in. Let's go ahead and shrink our function down by using Python's own * and ** tools, which allow us to accept arbitrary lists and dictionaries from the command line:

```
def hyper_cmd(cmd, *arg, **kwarg):
    '''
    Execute an arbitrary command on Minions which run hypervisors
    '''
    client = salt.client.get_local_client(__opts__['conf_file'])

    return client.cmd(
        hypers(client),
        cmd,
        arg=arg,
        kwarg=kwarg,
        expr_form='list',
        timeout=__opts__['timeout']
    )
```

Now we can run the following command:

```
# salt-run scan.hyper_cmd test.kwarg iface='wlp3s0'
```

The final module

With all of our code in place, the final module will look like:

```
'''
Scan Minions for various pieces of information

This file should be saved as salt/runners/scan.py
'''
import salt.client
import salt.key


__func_alias__ = {
    'up_': 'up'
}

def up_(tgt='*', tgt_type='glob'):
    '''
    Return a list of minions which are responding
    '''
    client = salt.client.get_local_client(__opts__['conf_file'])
    minions = client.cmd(
        tgt,
        'test.ping',
        expr_form=tgt_type,
        timeout=__opts__['timeout']
    '''
    Return a list of minions which are NOT responding
    '''
    minions = up_(tgt, tgt_type)

    key = salt.key.Key(__opts__)
    keys = key.list_keys()

    return sorted(set(keys['minions']) - set(minions))


def hypers(client=None):
    '''
```

```
    Return a list of Minions that are running hypervisors
    '''
    if client is None:
        client = salt.client.get_local_client(__opts__['conf_file'])

    minions = client.cmd(
        '*',
        'virt.is_hyper',
        timeout=__opts__['timeout']
    )

    hypers = []
    for minion in minions:
        if minions[minion] is True:
            hypers.append(minion)

    return hypers


def hyper_os():
    '''
    Return a list of which operating system each hypervisor is running
    '''
    client = salt.client.get_local_client(__opts__['conf_file'])

    return client.cmd(
        hypers(client),
        'grains.item',
        arg=('os',),
        expr_form='list',
        timeout=__opts__['timeout']
    )


def hyper_cmd(cmd, *arg, **kwarg):
    '''
    Execute an arbitrary command on Minions which run hypervisors
    '''
    client = salt.client.get_local_client(__opts__['conf_file'])

    return client.cmd(
        hypers(client),
        cmd,
        arg=arg,
```

```
            kwarg=kwarg,
            expr_form='list',
            timeout=__opts__['timeout']
    )
```

Troubleshooting runners

In a way, runners are a little easier to troubleshoot than other types of modules. For instance, even though they run on the Master, they don't need the `salt-master` service to be restarted to pick up new changes. In fact, unless you're using the local client, you don't actually have to have the `salt-master` service running.

Working with the salt-master service

If you are using the local client, and you try to issue a command without the `salt-master` service running, you will get an error that looks like this:

```
# salt-run scan.hyper_os
Exception occurred in runner scan.hyper_os: Traceback (most recent call last):
  File "/usr/lib/python2.7/site-packages/salt/client/mixins.py", line 340, in low
    data['return'] = self.functions[fun](*args, **kwargs)
  File "/usr/lib/python2.7/site-packages/salt/runners/scan.py", line 68, in hyper_os
    hypers(client),
  File "/usr/lib/python2.7/site-packages/salt/runners/scan.py", line 50, in hypers
    timeout=__opts__['timeout']
  File "/usr/lib/python2.7/site-packages/salt/client/__init__.py", line 562, in cmd
    **kwargs)
  File "/usr/lib/python2.7/site-packages/salt/client/__init__.py", line 317, in run_job
    raise SaltClientError(general_exception)
SaltClientError: Salt request timed out. The master is not responding. If this error persists after verifying the master is up, worker_threads may need to be increased.
```

This is because, although runners themselves don't rely on the `salt-master` service, Minions do rely on it to receive commands, and send responses back to the Master.

Timeout issues

If the Master is running properly and you're not receiving the responses that you expect, think about the targets that you're hitting. It is very common for a runner to issue commands to all Minions, but if you're testing in a large infrastructure, or you have keys on your Master that belong to Minions which are inaccessible or no longer exist, then runner commands can take a long time to return.

While writing your modules, you may want to consider changing the target from `'*'` to one specific Minion, or perhaps to a specific list of Minions (with the `expr_form` set to `'list'`, as we did in our `hyper_os()` and `hyper_cmd()` functions). Just make sure you set it back before you push it into production.

Summary

Runners add a scripting element to Salt, using Python. They are designed to run on the Master, but do not require the `salt-master` service to be running, unless they are using the local client to issue commands to Minions. Runners are designed to manage targeting on their own, but you can add elements to allow users to specify targets anyway. They are especially useful for using the output from one job as input for another job, which allows you to wrap your own logic around execution modules.

In the next chapter, we will allow the Master to use external sources to store the files that it serves to its Minions. Next up: adding external file servers.

8
Adding External File Servers

Salt Master normally keeps its resources locally on the machine that hosts it. This involves, among other things, files that are served to Minions. The file server loader allows you to use an external resource to store those files, and treat them as if they are local to the Master. In this chapter, we'll discuss:

- Understanding how Salt uses files
- Abstracting external sources to deliver files to Salt
- Using Salt's cache system
- Troubleshooting external file servers

How Salt uses files

There are two ways that Salt's built-in file server uses files when communicating with Minions. They can be served whole and intact, or they can be processed by a templating engine, using a renderer module as discussed in *Chapter 5, Rendering Data*.

In either case, these files are stored in one or more sets of directories, as configured with the `file_roots` directive in the master configuration file. These directories are grouped by environment. When Salt is looking for a file, it will search through the directories in the order in which they are listed. The default environment, `base`, normally uses `/srv/salt/` to store files. Such a configuration would look like:

```
file_roots:
  base:
    - /srv/salt/
```

What many users don't realize is that the `file_roots` directive is actually a configuration option that is specific to a file server module called `roots`. This module, along with all other file server modules, is configured using the `fileserver_backend` directive:

```
fileserver_backend:
  - roots
```

This is where you configure any other file server modules to be used within Salt. Once again, modules are configured in the order in which they are to be used. When the Master requests a file for a Minion, Salt will check with each of these modules until it finds a match. When it does, it will stop looking, and serve the file that it has found. That means that if you have the following configuration:

```
fileserver_backend:
  - git
  - roots
```

And Salt finds the requested file inside of Git, it will ignore any files that would otherwise be found on the local filesystem.

Mimicking a filesystem

If you have ever written a FUSE filesystem before, you will recognize some of the functions used inside a Salt file server module. Many of the operations used to request a file from an operating system are very similar to the files used by Salt to request a file. When it comes down to it, a Salt file server module is effectively a virtual filesystem, but with an API designed specifically for Salt, rather than for an operating system.

As you do development with file server modules, you may also notice another trend. While the data that is used may be stored in a remote location, it may be costly in terms of resources to repeatedly retrieve those files. Because of this, a number of file server modules will retrieve files from that remote location and then cache them locally on the Master, only updating them as necessary.

In this respect, when you are writing a file server module, you are often only implementing a means of retrieving and caching files, and serving them from the cache. This is not always the best thing to do; a truly dynamic file server based purely on database queries might perform best by always performing a lookup. You need to decide from the beginning what the most appropriate strategy is.

Looking at each function

The file server that we will be writing will be based on SFTP. Because SFTP calls can be expensive to make, we will use a caching implementation that relies on a popular Python library called Paramiko to retrieve files. For simplicity, we will only allow one SFTP server to be configured, but if you find yourself using this module, you may want to consider allowing multiple endpoints to be configured.

Setting up our module

Before we go over the functions that are used, we start setting up the module itself. We will implement a few functions that provide objects that we will use throughout the rest of our module:

```
'''
The backend for serving files from an SFTP account.

To enable, add ``sftp`` to the :conf_master:`fileserver_backend`
option in the
Master config file.

.. code-block:: yaml

    fileserver_backend:
      - sftp

Each environment is configured as a directory inside the SFTP account.
The name
of the directory must match the name of the environment.

.. code-block:: yaml

    sftpfs_host: sftp.example.com
    sftpfs_port: 22
    sftpfs_username: larry
    sftpfs_password: 123pass
    sftpfs_root: /srv/sftp/salt/
'''
import os
import os.path
import logging
import time
import salt.fileserver
import salt.utils
```

```python
import salt.syspaths

try:
    import fcntl
    HAS_FCNTL = True
except ImportError:
    HAS_FCNTL = False

try:
    import paramiko
    from paramiko import AuthenticationException
    HAS_LIBS = True
except ImportError:
    HAS_LIBS = False


__virtualname__ = 'sftp'

log = logging.getLogger()

transport = None
client = None


def __virtual__():
    '''
    Only load if proper conditions are met
    '''
    if __virtualname__ not in __opts__['fileserver_backend']:
        return False

    if not HAS_LIBS:
        return False

    if __opts__.get('sftpfs_root', None) is None:
        return False

    global client
    global transport

    host = __opts__.get('sftpfs_host')
    port = __opts__.get('sftpfs_port', 22)
    username = __opts__.get('sftpfs_username')
    password = __opts__.get('sftpfs_password')
    try:
```

```
        transport = paramiko.Transport((host, port))
        transport.connect(username=username, password=password)
        client = paramiko.SFTPClient.from_transport(transport)
    except AuthenticationException:
        return False


    return True
```

There's quite a bit going on already! Fortunately, you should recognize most of this by now, so this part should go by quickly.

We've included a docstring that's a bit longer than usual, but which explains how to configure Salt to use our module. We will see these parameters used when we get to the __virtual__() function.

Next, we set up our imports. The usage of most of these will be covered as we go through individual functions, but there are a couple that we have wrapped in try/except blocks. The first of these is fcntl, which is a Unix system call that handles file descriptors. This library is useful for locking files in Unix and Linux, but does not exist in Windows. However, the rest of our module is usable in Windows, so we set a flag now that can be used later, when we need to lock files.

The second import is Paramiko. This is one of the most popular connection libraries available for SSH and SFTP in Python, and simple to use for our purposes. If it has not been installed, then we can return False in the __virtual__() function.

We've added __virtualname__, even though it's not strictly necessary, just so that we have a central and easy-to-find place to name our module. We will use this variable in the __virtual__() function. We've also added a little logging, which we'll make use of.

Before even loading the __virtual__() function, we've defined two variables to be used for connecting to the SFTP server. We'll assign a connection to them inside __virtual__(), and it will be used throughout the rest of the module.

Finally, we have our __virtual__() function. First, we check to see if our module has even been configured for use. If not, there's no point in going any further. We also check to make sure Paramiko is installed. Then we make sure a root directory has been specified for the SFTP server. It's not evident now, but this directory will be required elsewhere. If it's not there, then we're not even going to bother trying to connect to the server.

If it is defined, then we can go ahead and try to make our connection. Paramiko will raise AuthenticationException if the rest of our parameters have been incorrectly defined, and in that case of course, we will consider this module unavailable and return False. But if all of those stars line up, then we're ready for business!

Let's go over the functions that we should find inside any given file server module. In each section, we will implement and explain that function.

envs()

We start off by reporting which environments have been configured for this file server. At the very least, the base environment should be supported and reported, but it's best to offer a mechanism to support other environments as well. Because we're effectively abstracting a file management mechanism, it's often easiest to just do this by separating environments into directories:

```
def envs():
    '''
    Treat each directory as an environment
    '''
    ret = []
    root = __opts__.get('sftpfs_root')
    for entry in client.listdir_attr(root):
        if str(oct(entry.st_mode)).startswith('04'):
            ret.append(entry.filename)
    return ret
```

This function needs to return a list. Because we've separated out environments into their own directories, all that we need to do for our module is return a list of directories at the root directory that we've configured.

This function is tricky to test, because there's no direct interface for it in any Salt modules. However, it can be tested once the next two functions are in place.

file_list() and dir_list()

These two functions are pretty self-explanatory; they connect to the remote endpoint and return a list of all files and directories for that environment:

```
def file_list(load):
    '''
    Return a list of all files on the file server in a specified
    environment
    '''
```

```
        root = __opts__.get('sftpfs_root')
        path = os.path.join(root, load['saltenv'], load['prefix'])
        return _recur_path(path, load['saltenv'])


    def dir_list(load):
        '''
        Return a list of all directories on the master
        '''
        root = __opts__.get('sftpfs_root')
        path = os.path.join(root, load['saltenv'], load['prefix'])
        return _recur_path(path, load['saltenv'], True)


    def _recur_path(path, saltenv, only_dirs=False):
        '''
        Recurse through the remote directory structure
        '''
        root = __opts__.get('sftpfs_root')
        ret = []
        try:
            for entry in client.listdir_attr(path):
                full = os.path.join(path, entry.filename)
                if str(oct(entry.st_mode)).startswith('04'):
                    ret.append(full)
                    ret.extend(_recur_path(full, saltenv, only_dirs))
                else:
                    if only_dirs is False:
                        ret.append(full)
            return ret
        except IOError:
            return []
```

What is needed by these two functions is exactly the same, except for whether or not to include files. Because recursion is usually needed anyway, we've added a recursive function called `_recur_path()` that can report either just directories or both files and directories. You may notice the check against `entry.st_mode`. You may think of a Unix file mode as a set of permissions, which can be changed using the `chmod` (**change mode**) command. However, the mode also stores which kind of file it is:

```
0100755  # This is a file, with 0755 permissions
040755  # This is a directory, with 0755 permissions
```

We could use another try/except block to see if we can descend into a directory. But it's a little less work to check the mode. If it starts with `04`, then we know that it is a directory.

Each of these functions requires a `load` argument. If you were to look inside, you would find a dictionary that looks like this:

```
{'cmd': '_file_list', 'prefix': '', 'saltenv': 'base'}
```

The `cmd` field stores what kind of command was used. `prefix` will contain the directory path, inside the environment, which contains any requested files, and `saltenv` tells you the name of the requested environment itself. You will see this argument throughout the module, but it looks largely the same.

Let's go ahead and look at a couple of Salt commands:

```
# salt-call --local cp.list_master
local:
    - testdir
    - testfile
# salt-call --local cp.list_master_dirs
local:
    - testdir
```

Keep in mind that `--local` will tell `salt-call` to pretend that it is its own Master. In that case, it will look to the `minion` configuration file for the connection parameters.

find_file()

Like `file_list()` and `dir_list()`, this function checks a requested path. It then reports whether or not the specified file exists:

```
    '''
    def find_file(path, saltenv='base', **kwargs):
        '''
        Search the environment for the relative path
        '''
        fnd = {'path': '',
               'rel': ''}

        full = os.path.join(salt.syspaths.CACHE_DIR, 'sftpfs',
        saltenv, path)
```

```
    if os.path.isfile(full) and not
    salt.fileserver.is_file_ignored(__opts__, full):
        fnd['path'] = full
        fnd['rel'] = path

    return fnd
```

You may have noticed that no SFTP calls are being made in this function. That's because we're using a caching file server, and all that we need to check for right now is to see if the file has been cached. If it has, then Salt will just serve the file from the cache.

If you are writing a file server module that does not keep a local cache, then this function should check the remote endpoint to ensure that the file exists.

Speaking of the cache, one of the more important lines in this function is the one that defines the `full` variable. This sets up the directory structure that is to be used for this caching file server. It makes use of `salt.syspaths` to determine the correct directory for your platform; normally, this will be `/var/cache/salt/`.

Note that a `load` is not passed into this function, but `saltenv` that would normally be in the `load` is. Previous versions of Salt passed in `saltenv` as just `env`, and the `**kwargs` functions as a catch-all to keep Python from choking on old implementations.

Once again, there is no way to test this function directly. It will be used by the `update()` function later on in this section.

serve_file()

Once a file has been found using `find_file()`, its data is passed to this function in order to return the actual file contents:

```
def serve_file(load, fnd):
    '''
    Return a chunk from a file based on the data received
    '''
    ret = {'data': '',
           'dest': ''}

    if 'path' not in load or 'loc' not in load or 'saltenv' not in
    load:
        return ret
```

```
        if not fnd['path']:
            return ret

    ret['dest'] = fnd['rel']
    gzip = load.get('gzip', None)

    full = os.path.join(salt.syspaths.CACHE_DIR, 'sftpfs',
    fnd['path'])

    with salt.utils.fopen(fnd['path'], 'rb') as fp_:
        fp_.seek(load['loc'])
        data = fp_.read(__opts__['file_buffer_size'])
        if gzip and data:
            data = salt.utils.gzip_util.compress(data, gzip)
            ret['gzip'] = gzip
        ret['data'] = data
    return ret
```

This function is used directly by Salt's own internal file server, which splits files into chunks before delivering them to Minions. If the gzip flag is set to True in the master configuration file, then each of these chunks will be individually compressed.

Since, in our case, this function is serving files from the cache, you can probably get away with using this function as it is printed here, except for the line that defines the full variable. If you are not using a caching file server, then you will need to have a way to access and deliver each chunk of a file, as requested.

You can test this function using the cp.get_file function. This function requires both a filename to download, and a full path to save the file locally:

```
# salt-call --local cp.get_file salt://testfile /tmp/testfile
local:
    /tmp/testfile
```

update()

At regular intervals, Salt will request that an external file server perform maintenance on itself. This function will compare the local file cache (if it is being used) with the remote endpoint, and update Salt with new information:

```
    def update():
        '''
        Update the cache, and reap old entries
        '''
```

```
base_dir = os.path.join(salt.syspaths.CACHE_DIR, 'sftpfs')
if not os.path.isdir(base_dir):
    os.makedirs(base_dir)

try:
    salt.fileserver.reap_fileserver_cache_dir(
        os.path.join(base_dir, 'hash'),
        find_file
    )
except (IOError, OSError):
    # Hash file won't exist if no files have yet been served
    up
    pass

# Find out what the latest file is, so that we only update
files more
# recent than that, and not the entire filesystem
if os.listdir(base_dir):
    all_files = []
    for root, subFolders, files in os.walk(base_dir):
        for fn_ in files:
            full_path = os.path.join(root, fn_)
            all_files.append([
                os.path.getmtime(full_path),
                full_path,
            ])

# Pull in any files that have changed
for env in envs():
    path = os.path.join(__opts__['sftpfs_root'], env)
    result = client.listdir_attr(path)
    for fileobj in result:
        file_name = os.path.join(base_dir, env,
        fileobj.filename)

        # Make sure the directory exists first
        comps = file_name.split('/')
        file_path = '/'.join(comps[:-1])
        if not os.path.exists(file_path):
            os.makedirs(file_path)

        if str(oct(fileobj.st_mode)).startswith('04'):
            # Create the directory
            if not os.path.exists(file_name):
```

```
                os.makedirs(file_name)
        else:
            # Write out the file
            if fileobj.st_mtime > all_files[file_name]:
                client.get(os.path.join(path,
                    fileobj.filename), file_name)
        os.utime(file_name, (fileobj.st_atime,
            fileobj.st_mtime))
```

Whew! This is a long one! First, we define the cache directory, and if it is not there, then we create it. This is important for caching file servers. Then we ask Salt to clean up old entries, using the built-in `salt.fileserver.reap_fileserver_cache_dir()` function. This passes in a reference to `find_file()` to help with the work.

The next section walks through the remaining files to check their timestamps. Files will only be downloaded if they either have not yet been downloaded, or if there is a more recent copy on the remote SFTP server.

Finally, we loop through each environment to see which files have changed, and download them if necessary. Any directories that don't exist in the local cache will be created. And whether we create a file or a directory, we make sure to update its timestamp so that the cache matches what's on the server.

This function will be run periodically by the Salt Master, but you can force it to run by manually deleting a file from the local cache, and then requesting a copy:

```
# rm /var/cache/salt/sftpfs/base/testfile
# salt-call --local cp.get_file salt://testfile /tmp/testfile
local:
    /tmp/testfile
```

file_hash()

One of the ways that Salt knows that a file has been changed is by keeping track of the file's hash signature. If a hash changes, then Salt will know that it is time to serve a new copy of the file from the cache:

```
def file_hash(load, fnd):
    '''
    Return a file hash, the hash type is set in the master config
    file
    '''
    path = fnd['path']
    ret = {}
```

```
# if the file doesn't exist, we can't get a hash
if not path or not os.path.isfile(path):
    return ret

# set the hash_type as it is determined by config
ret['hash_type'] = __opts__['hash_type']

# Check if the hash is cached
# Cache file's contents should be 'hash:mtime'
cache_path = os.path.join(
    salt.syspaths.CACHE_DIR,
    'sftpfs',
    'hash',
    load['saltenv'],
    '{0}.hash.{1}'.format(
        fnd['rel'],
        ret['hash_type']
    )
)

# If we have a cache, serve that if the mtime hasn't changed
if os.path.exists(cache_path):
    try:
        with salt.utils.fopen(cache_path, 'rb') as fp_:
            try:
                hsum, mtime = fp_.read().split(':')
            except ValueError:
                log.debug(
                    'Fileserver attempted to read incomplete
                    cache file. Retrying.'
                )
                file_hash(load, fnd)
                return ret
            if os.path.getmtime(path) == mtime:
                # check if mtime changed
                ret['hsum'] = hsum
                return ret
    except os.error:
        # Can't use Python select() because we need Windows
        support
        log.debug(
            'Fileserver encountered lock when reading cache
            file. Retrying.'
        )
```

```
                file_hash(load, fnd)
                return ret

        # If we don't have a cache entry-- lets make one
        ret['hsum'] = salt.utils.get_hash(path, __opts__['hash_type'])
        cache_dir = os.path.dirname(cache_path)

        # Make cache directory if it doesn't exist
        if not os.path.exists(cache_dir):
            os.makedirs(cache_dir)

        # Save the cache object 'hash:mtime'
        if HAS_FCNTL:
            with salt.utils.flopen(cache_path, 'w') as fp_:
                fp_.write('{0}:{1}'.format(ret['hsum'],
                os.path.getmtime(path)))
                fcntl.flock(fp_.fileno(), fcntl.LOCK_UN)
            return ret
        else:
            with salt.utils.fopen(cache_path, 'w') as fp_:
                fp_.write('{0}:{1}'.format(ret['hsum'],
                os.path.getmtime(path)))
            return ret
```

This is the longest function in our example, but thankfully it also needs the least amount of modification, for a caching file server. As with the other examples in this book, you can download a copy of this module from Packt Publishing's website. Once you have it downloaded, you will likely only need to change the value of cache_path. However, we will go through this function briefly anyway.

After setting up a few basics, including the path of the file being hashed, check for the existence of said path, and define where in the cache to keep a copy of the hash. In our case, we've set up another directory structure inside the cache, mirroring the original, but with .hash.<hash_type> appended to the filename. Resulting files will have names like this:

```
/var/cache/salt/sftpfs/hash/base/testfile.hash.md5
```

The next section checks to see if the hash file has been created, and if so, whether or not the timestamp matches the local copy. If the timestamp on the existing hash file is too old, then a new hash will be generated.

If we get past all of that, then we know it's time to generate a new hash. After determining the hash type to use and setting up a directory to put it in, we get to the section that actually writes the hash to disk. Remember the check for `fcntl` at the beginning of the module? On a busy Salt Master, it's possible that multiple attempts may be made simultaneously to work on the same file. With `fcntl` in place, we can lock that file before writing to it, to avoid corruption.

The final module

With all of our functions in place, the final module will look like this:

```
'''
The backend for serving files from an SFTP account.

To enable, add ``sftp`` to the :conf_master:`fileserver_backend`
option in the
Master config file.

.. code-block:: yaml

    fileserver_backend:
      - sftp

Each environment is configured as a directory inside the SFTP account.
The name
of the directory must match the name of the environment.

.. code-block:: yaml

    sftpfs_host: sftp.example.com
    sftpfs_port: 22
    sftpfs_username: larry
    sftpfs_password: 123pass
    sftpfs_root: /srv/sftp/salt/
'''
import os
import os.path
import logging
import time
```

```
try:
    import fcntl
    HAS_FCNTL = True
except ImportError:
    # fcntl is not available on windows
    HAS_FCNTL = False

import salt.fileserver
import salt.utils
import salt.syspaths

try:
    import paramiko
    from paramiko import AuthenticationException
    HAS_LIBS = True
except ImportError:
    HAS_LIBS = False


__virtualname__ = 'sftp'

log = logging.getLogger()

transport = None
client = None


def __virtual__():
    '''
    Only load if proper conditions are met
    '''
    if __virtualname__ not in __opts__['fileserver_backend']:
        return False

    if not HAS_LIBS:
        return False

    if __opts__.get('sftpfs_root', None) is None:
        return False

    global client
    global transport

    host = __opts__.get('sftpfs_host')
    port = __opts__.get('sftpfs_port', 22)
```

```
        username = __opts__.get('sftpfs_username')
        password = __opts__.get('sftpfs_password')
        try:
            transport = paramiko.Transport((host, port))
            transport.connect(username=username, password=password)
            client = paramiko.SFTPClient.from_transport(transport)
        except AuthenticationException:
            return False

        return True


    def envs():
        '''
        Treat each directory as an environment
        '''
        ret = []
        root = __opts__.get('sftpfs_root')
        for entry in client.listdir_attr(root):
            if str(oct(entry.st_mode)).startswith('04'):
                ret.append(entry.filename)
        return ret


    def file_list(load):
        '''
        Return a list of all files on the file server in a specified
        environment
        '''
        root = __opts__.get('sftpfs_root')
        path = os.path.join(root, load['saltenv'], load['prefix'])
        return _recur_path(path, load['saltenv'])


    def dir_list(load):
        '''
        Return a list of all directories on the master
        '''
        root = __opts__.get('sftpfs_root')
        path = os.path.join(root, load['saltenv'], load['prefix'])
        return _recur_path(path, load['saltenv'], True)
```

```
def _recur_path(path, saltenv, only_dirs=False):
    '''
    Recurse through the remote directory structure
    '''
    root = __opts__.get('sftpfs_root')
    ret = []
    try:
        for entry in client.listdir_attr(path):
            full = os.path.join(path, entry.filename)
            if str(oct(entry.st_mode)).startswith('04'):
                ret.append(full)
                ret.extend(_recur_path(full, saltenv, only_dirs))
            else:
                if only_dirs is False:
                    ret.append(full)
        return ret
    except IOError:
        return []


def find_file(path, saltenv='base', env=None, **kwargs):
    '''
    Search the environment for the relative path
    '''
    fnd = {'path': '',
           'rel': ''}

    full = os.path.join(salt.syspaths.CACHE_DIR, 'sftpfs',
    saltenv, path)

    if os.path.isfile(full) and not
    salt.fileserver.is_file_ignored(__opts__, full):
        fnd['path'] = full
        fnd['rel'] = path

    return fnd


def serve_file(load, fnd):
    '''
    Return a chunk from a file based on the data received
    '''
    ret = {'data': '',
```

```
                    'dest': ''}

        if 'path' not in load or 'loc' not in load or 'saltenv' not in
        load:
            return ret

        if not fnd['path']:
            return ret

        ret['dest'] = fnd['rel']
        gzip = load.get('gzip', None)

        full = os.path.join(salt.syspaths.CACHE_DIR, 'sftpfs',
        fnd['path'])

        with salt.utils.fopen(fnd['path'], 'rb') as fp_:
            fp_.seek(load['loc'])
            data = fp_.read(__opts__['file_buffer_size'])
            if gzip and data:
                data = salt.utils.gzip_util.compress(data, gzip)
                ret['gzip'] = gzip
            ret['data'] = data
        return ret


def update():
    '''
    Update the cache, and reap old entries
    '''
    base_dir = os.path.join(salt.syspaths.CACHE_DIR, 'sftpfs')
    if not os.path.isdir(base_dir):
        os.makedirs(base_dir)

    try:
        salt.fileserver.reap_fileserver_cache_dir(
            os.path.join(base_dir, 'hash'),
            find_file
        )
    except (IOError, OSError):
        # Hash file won't exist if no files have yet been served
        up
        pass
```

```
    # Find out what the latest file is, so that we only update
    files more
    # recent than that, and not the entire filesystem
    if os.listdir(base_dir):
        all_files = {}
        for root, subFolders, files in os.walk(base_dir):
            for fn_ in files:
                full_path = os.path.join(root, fn_)
                all_files[full_path] = os.path.getmtime(full_path)

    # Pull in any files that have changed
    for env in envs():
        path = os.path.join(__opts__['sftpfs_root'], env)
        result = client.listdir_attr(path)
        for fileobj in result:
            file_name = os.path.join(base_dir, env,
            fileobj.filename)

            # Make sure the directory exists first
            comps = file_name.split('/')
            file_path = '/'.join(comps[:-1])
            if not os.path.exists(file_path):
                os.makedirs(file_path)

            if str(oct(fileobj.st_mode)).startswith('04'):
                # Create the directory
                if not os.path.exists(file_name):
                    os.makedirs(file_name)
            else:
                # Write out the file
                if fileobj.st_mtime > all_files[file_name]:
                    client.get(os.path.join(path,
                    fileobj.filename), file_name)
            os.utime(file_name, (fileobj.st_atime,
            fileobj.st_mtime))


def file_hash(load, fnd):
    '''
    Return a file hash, the hash type is set in the master config
    file
    '''
    path = fnd['path']
    ret = {}
```

```
# if the file doesn't exist, we can't get a hash
if not path or not os.path.isfile(path):
    return ret


# set the hash_type as it is determined by config
# -- so mechanism won't change that
ret['hash_type'] = __opts__['hash_type']


# Check if the hash is cached
# Cache file's contents should be 'hash:mtime'
cache_path = os.path.join(
    salt.syspaths.CACHE_DIR,
    'sftpfs',
    'hash',
    load['saltenv'],
    '{0}.hash.{1}'.format(
        fnd['rel'],
        ret['hash_type']
    )
)


# If we have a cache, serve that if the mtime hasn't changed
if os.path.exists(cache_path):
    try:
        with salt.utils.fopen(cache_path, 'rb') as fp_:
            try:
                hsum, mtime = fp_.read().split(':')
            except ValueError:
                log.debug(
                    'Fileserver attempted to read'
                    'incomplete cache file. Retrying.'
                )
                file_hash(load, fnd)
                return ret
            if os.path.getmtime(path) == mtime:
                # check if mtime changed
                ret['hsum'] = hsum
                return ret
    except os.error:
        # Can't use Python select() because we need Windows
        support
        log.debug(
            'Fileserver encountered lock when reading cache
            file. Retrying.'
```

```
        )
        file_hash(load, fnd)
        return ret

    # If we don't have a cache entry-- lets make one
    ret['hsum'] = salt.utils.get_hash(path, __opts__['hash_type'])
    cache_dir = os.path.dirname(cache_path)

    # Make cache directory if it doesn't exist
    if not os.path.exists(cache_dir):
        os.makedirs(cache_dir)

    # Save the cache object 'hash:mtime'
    if HAS_FCNTL:
        with salt.utils.flopen(cache_path, 'w') as fp_:
            fp_.write('{0}:{1}'.format(ret['hsum'],
            os.path.getmtime(path)))
            fcntl.flock(fp_.fileno(), fcntl.LOCK_UN)
        return ret
    else:
        with salt.utils.fopen(cache_path, 'w') as fp_:
            fp_.write('{0}:{1}'.format(ret['hsum'], os.path.
getmtime(path)))
        return ret
```

Troubleshooting file servers

File server modules can be tricky to troubleshoot, because so many of the pieces
need to be in place before others are usable. But there are some tricks that you
can keep in mind.

Start small

I've tried to present the functions that are necessary, in the order that is easiest
for writing and troubleshooting. While envs() cannot be called directly, it is easy
to write, and can be debugged while working on file_list() and dir_list().
And those two functions are easy to troubleshoot using the cp.list_master and
cp.list_master_dirs functions, respectively.

Test on a Minion

While file server modules are designed to be used on the Master, it is possible to test them on a Minion. Be sure to define all of the appropriate configurations in the `minion` configuration file instead of the `master` file. Use `salt-call --local` to issue commands, and regularly wipe both the local cache (in `/var/salt/cache/`) and any files that were downloaded using `cp.get_file`.

Summary

File server modules can be used to present resources on an external endpoint as if they were files sitting on the Master. The default file server module, called `roots`, does in fact use local files on the Master. Many file server modules cache files locally on the Master, to avoid making too many calls to the external source, but this is not always appropriate.

There are a number of functions inside a file server module, which work in concert to present a file-server-like interface. Some of these functions cannot be tested directly, but they can still be tested in tandem with other functions that do have a direct external interface.

Despite all of the functions involved, file server modules are relatively easy to write. In the next chapter, we'll talk about cloud modules, which have even more required functions, but which are even easier to write.

9
Connecting to the Cloud

Cloud modules may seem like the most daunting type of Salt module, because of how many functions are required to present a cohesive tool for a cloud provider. Fortunately, connecting to most cloud providers is easy, once you know how. In this chapter, we'll discuss:

- Understanding how cloud components fit together
- Learning which functions are required, and how they are used
- Comparing Libcloud-based modules with direct REST modules
- Writing a generic cloud module
- Troubleshooting cloud modules

Understanding cloud components

The word *cloud* has suffered from an unfortunate bout of overuse and misuse in recent years, so before we talk about what the components look like, we need to define what we're actually talking about in the first place.

Salt Cloud is designed to operate with *compute cloud* providers. This means that they offer computing resources, often in the form of virtual machines. A number of cloud providers also offer other resources, such as storage space, DNS, and load balancing. While Salt Cloud isn't explicitly designed to manage these resources, it is possible to add support for them.

For our purposes, we will discuss creating cloud drivers with a focus on managing virtual machines. Some of the techniques can be used for adding other resources, so if you're planning on going in that direction, this chapter will still be useful to you.

Looking at the puzzle pieces

The primary goal of Salt Cloud is to easily create virtual machines on a cloud provider, install a Salt Minion onto that machine, and then automatically accept that Minion's keys on the Master. When you dig down, you will find that a number of pieces fit together to achieve this goal.

Connection mechanism

Most cloud providers offer an API to manage the resources in your account. This API comprises an authentication scheme, and a collection of URLs that are used in similar ways. Almost every cloud provider supports URLs based on both GET and POST methods, but some support other methods such as PATCH and DELETE.

Quite frequently, these URLs will include up to four components:

- A resource name
- The action to be performed on that resource
- The ID of the resource to be managed
- Arguments that define how the resource is managed

These components can be combined with the authentication scheme to create a single tool that is used to perform all of the management features that are available.

Listing resources

Most resources have a way to list them from the API. These include both options that are defined by the cloud provider and resources that belong to your account and can be managed by you. Some of the resources that can usually be listed from the API are:

- Operating system images
- Sizes of virtual machines that can be created
- Existing virtual machines in a user's account
- Details about specific virtual machines
- Non-compute resources that are managed by the account

A Salt Cloud module should provide a few different ways to list resources, both for creating new virtual machines and for managing existing virtual machines.

Creating virtual machines

The most complex component of most cloud modules is the `create()` function, which orchestrates the tasks of requesting a virtual machine, waiting for it to become available, logging in to it and installing Salt, and accepting that virtual machine's Minion keys on the Master. Many of these tasks have been abstracted into helper functions that can be called from cloud modules, which greatly simplifies the development of the `create()` function.

Managing other resources

Once the preceding components have been put together, creating other functions to create, list, modify, and delete other resources will usually not take much effort.

Libcloud versus SDK versus direct REST API

There are three types of cloud modules that ship with Salt. The first and original type of module uses a library called Libcloud to communicate with cloud providers. Using this kind of library has some distinct advantages:

- Libcloud supports a huge amount of cloud providers
- Libcloud provides a standard and reasonably consistent interface across providers
- Salt Cloud has a number of functions built in specifically for Libcloud
- Libcloud is actively developed, with frequent releases

There are some disadvantages to using Libcloud:

- Not every feature in every cloud is supported by Libcloud
- New cloud providers may not yet be supported
- Old, obscure, and proprietary drivers may not ever be supported

Some cloud providers also provide their own libraries for connecting to their infrastructure. This may prove the fastest, easiest, or most reliable way to connect to them. Some advantages to using a provider's own SDK are:

- The developers are likely to have the most complete knowledge of the API
- When new features are released, the SDK is often the first library to support them

Some disadvantages are:

- Some SDKs still don't support all of the features for that cloud provider
- Some SDKs can be difficult to use

Another option for communicating with a cloud provider is to communicate directly with their REST API. Some advantages to this are:

- You control how the module is maintained
- You can make your own additions without waiting for new versions of a library

But there are some definite disadvantages to using a direct REST API:

- You have to maintain the module
- You have to add any new features yourself
- You aren't likely to have as many resources to use the driver as the cloud provider has

You are going to need to decide which of these options is most appropriate for your situation. Fortunately, once you have set up a connection mechanism to use (whether you write it yourself or use somebody else's), there aren't really any differences between the functions that make use of those connections.

Writing a generic cloud module

We're going to set up a very generic module that uses a direct REST API to communicate with a cloud provider. If you spend a lot of time with different APIs, you'll find the style used here to be very common.

Checking for required configuration

In order to use a cloud provider, you will need a `__virtual__()` function to check for required configuration, and if necessary, any dependencies. You will also need a function called `get_configured_provider()`, which checks to make sure that the configuration that is required to connect to your cloud provider (usually authentication at the very least, and sometimes other connection parameters) have been specified. We will also need to define `__virtualname__`, which contains the name of the driver as Salt Cloud will know it. Let's go ahead and start our cloud module with these:

```
'''
Generic Salt Cloud module
```

This module is not designed for any specific cloud provider, but is generic
enough that only minimal changes may be required for some providers.

This file should be saved as salt/cloud/clouds/generic.py

Set up the cloud configuration at ``/etc/salt/cloud.providers`` or
``/etc/salt/cloud.providers.d/generic.conf``:

.. code-block:: yaml

```
    my-cloud-config:
        driver: generic
        # The login user
        user: larry
        # The user's password
        password: 123pass
        # The user's API key
        api_key: 0123456789abcdef
'''
__virtualname__ = 'generic'


def __virtual__():
    '''
    Check for cloud configs
    '''
    # No special libraries required

    if get_configured_provider() is False:
        return False

    return __virtualname__


def get_configured_provider():
    '''
    Make sure configuration is correct
    '''
    return config.is_provider_configured(
        __opts__,
        __active_provider_name__ or __virtualname__,
        ('user', 'password', 'apikey')
    )
```

We've started out with a `docstring` that contains information about the required configuration for our driver. We're going to stick with a simple authentication scheme, which uses an API key as part of the URL, and an HTTP username and password.

The `__virtual__()` function should first make sure that any required libraries are installed. In our case, we don't need anything special, so we'll skip that part. We then call `get_configured_provider()` to make sure that any required configurations are in place, and if all is good, we return `__virtualname__`.

The `get_configured_provider()` function will never change, outside of the list of parameters that are absolutely required in order for the module to work. If you are going to accept any optional parameters, do not include them in this function.

> The `get_configured_provider()` function mentions another built-in variable called `__active_provider_name__`. This contains a combination of the name that the user sets for this module in their provider config (such as `my-cloud-config`) and the name of the actual driver itself (in our case, `generic`), separated by a colon (`:`). If you were to use the sample configuration in our docstring, then `__active_provider_name__` would be set to `my-cloud-config:generic`.

Using http.query()

Salt comes with its own library for communicating over HTTP. This library is not a connection library itself; rather, it allows you to use `urllib2` (which ships with Python), Tornado (which is a dependency of Salt itself), or `requests` (which is a very popular and powerful HTTP library for Python). Like Libcloud, Salt's HTTP library strives to provide a consistent interface across available libraries. You can specify which library is to be used, if you need to use specific features in that library, but by default Tornado is used.

This library lives in `salt.utils` and contains a number of HTTP-related functions. The one that is most commonly used is called `query()`. It not only supports all three backend libraries but also includes mechanisms to automatically translate return data from either JSON or XML into a Python dictionary.

A call to `http.query()` usually looks something like this:

```
import salt.utils.http
result = salt.utils.http.query(
    'https://api.example.com/v1/resource/action/id',
    'POST',
```

```
        data=post_data_dict,
        decode=True,
        decode_type='json',
        opts=__opts__
    )
print(result['dict'])
```

A common REST API

Before we connect to a REST API, we need to know what it looks like. The structure of the URL often contains the following components:

```
https://<hostname>/<version>/<resource>[/<action>[/<id>]]
```

Technically, the URL scheme can be HTTP, but if that's your only option, I would recommend switching to another cloud provider.

The hostname usually contains some hint that it belongs to the API, such as `api.example.com`. The documentation for your cloud provider will tell you which hostname to use here. The hostname may also include information about which data center you are communicating with, such as `eu-north.api.example.com`.

Most providers also require you to specify which version of their API you are using. This may be in the URL, or in the `POST` data, or even in the client request headers. You should always use the latest version unless you have a very good reason not to, but cloud providers will often support old versions as well, if only temporarily.

The resource refers to what you are actually monitoring. This may be something like `instance` or `nodes` for virtual machines, `storage` or `volumes` to refer to disks, or `images` to refer to prebuilt operating system images or templates. I wish I could be more specific here, but this will depend on your cloud provider.

The action may or may not appear in the URL. Some cloud providers will include actions such as `create`, `list`, `modify`, `delete`, and so on, followed by the ID of the resource to be managed, where necessary.

However, it's becoming increasingly common for the action to be determined by the HTTP method that is used to make the call. The following methods are commonly used by REST APIs:

GET

This is used for calls that will only display, but never change resources. If an ID is not given, then a list of resources is usually given. If an ID is used, then the details about that specific resource will be returned.

POST

This is often used for calls that create data, and frequently for those that modify data. If an ID is not declared, then a new resource will usually be created. If an ID is given, then an existing resource will be modified.

PATCH

This method was recently added for modifying existing resources. If a cloud provider makes use of this method, then they are unlikely to allow POST to modify existing data. Instead, POST will only be used to apply new data, and PATCH will be used to update existing data.

DELETE

Calls using a DELETE method will generally include both a resource type, and the ID of the resource to be removed. This method is never used to create or modify data; only remove it.

Setting up a _query() function

Now that we know what the API will look like, let's create a function to communicate with it. We will make use of http.query() to talk to it, but we also need to wrap a few other items in there as well. We'll start with a function declaration:

```
def _query(
    resource=None,
    action=None,
    method='GET',
    location=None,
    data=None,
):
```

Notice that we have made this function private. There is no reason to allow this function to be called directly from the command line, so we need to hide it. We have allowed any of the arguments to remain unspecified, because we won't always need all of them.

Let's go ahead and set our _query() function, and then go over each of the components in it:

```
import json
import salt.utils.http
```

```python
import salt.config as config


def _query(
        resource=None,
        action=None,
        params=None,
        method='GET',
        data=None
    ):
    '''
    Make a web call to the cloud provider
    '''
    user = config.get_cloud_config_value(
        'user', get_configured_provider(), __opts__,
    )

    password = config.get_cloud_config_value(
        'password', get_configured_provider(), __opts__,
    )

    api_key = config.get_cloud_config_value(
        'api_key', get_configured_provider(), __opts__,
    )

    location = config.get_cloud_config_value(
        'location', get_configured_provider(), __opts__,
        default=None
    )

    if location is None:
        location = 'eu-north'

    url = 'https://{0}.api.example.com/v1'.format(location)

    if resource:
        url += '/{0}'.format(resource)

    if action:
        url += '/{0}'.format(action)

    if not isinstance(params, dict):
        params = {}
```

```
        params['api_key'] = api_key

        if data is not None:
            data = json.dumps(data)

        result = salt.utils.http.query(
            url,
            method,
            params=params,
            data=data,
            decode=True,
            decode_type='json',
            hide_fields=['api_key'],
            opts=__opts__,
        )

        return result['dict']
```

We start off by collecting the connection parameters that are required for our cloud provider. The `salt.config` library includes a function called `get_cloud_config_value()` that searches through the cloud configuration for the requested value. It can search through the main cloud configuration (usually at `/etc/salt/cloud`) as well as through any provider or profile configuration. In this case, all of the configuration should be found in the provider configuration, as specified in our docstring.

Once we have collected the `user`, `password`, and `api_key`, we turn our attention to `location`. You may recall that many cloud providers use the hostname to differentiate different data centers. Many also have a default data center. In the case of our generic driver, we'll assume that `eu-north` is the default, and create a URL using that. Our URL also contains a version, as we mentioned before.

We then look at the resource that will be used, and any actions that will be performed on it. If found, these will be appended to the URL path. With those in place, we look at any parameters that will be added to the URL.

The `params` variable refers to `<name>=<value>` pairs that will be added to the URL. These will start with a question mark (?) and then be separated with an ampersand (&), for instance:

```
http://example.com/form.cgi?name1=value1&name2=value2&name3=value3
```

Instead of appending these to the URL by ourselves, we'll let the `http.query()` function take care of it for us. It will properly encode this data if specified and append it to the end of the URL for us.

If used, `params` need to be specified as a dictionary. We know that `api_key` will be one `params`, so we add it after doing a type check.

Finally, we need to look at any data that is going to be `POST`ed to the cloud provider. Many providers require `POST` data to be sent as a JSON string, rather than as URL-encoded data, so if any data is given, we'll convert it to JSON before sending it over.

Once we have everything prepared, we use `http.query()` (as `salt.utils.http.query()`) to actually make the call. You can see `url`, `method` (as specified in the function declaration), `params`, and `data`. We've also set `decode` to `True` and `decode_type` to `json`, so that the return data from the cloud provider will automatically be converted to a dictionary for us.

We've also passed through a list of fields to hide from any logging that may occur inside the `http.query()` function. This will keep data such as our `api_key` private, in the event that any logs are generated. Rather than logging a URL such as:

```
https://example.com/?api_key=0123456789abcdef
```

A sanitized URL will be logged:

```
https://example.com/?api_key=XXXXXXXXXX
```

Finally, we pass through a copy of `__opts__`, so that `http.query()` has access to any variables that it needs from the `master` or `minion` configuration files.

The `http.query()` function will return a dictionary, including an item called `dict`, which contains the return data from the cloud provider, converted into a dictionary. This is what we will pass back to any functions calling our `_query()` function.

Getting profile details

Once we have the ability to connect to a cloud provider, we need to be able to collect information that can be used to create a VM on that provider. That almost always includes a list of VM images and VM sizes. If a cloud provider has multiple data centers (and most of them do), then you will also need a function that returns a list of them.

These three functions are called `avail_images()`, `avail_sizes()`, and `avail_locations()`. They are accessed from the `salt-cloud` command using the `--list-images`, `--list-sizes`, and `--list-locations` options, respectively.

Listing images

Images refer to a prebuilt root VM volume. With Windows images, this will be the `c:\` disk volume. In other operating systems, it will be the `/` volume. Very commonly, a cloud provider will give access to a number of different operating systems, and a number of different versions of each of those.

For instance, a cloud provider may offer a single image each for Ubuntu 14.04, Ubuntu 14.10, Ubuntu 15.04, and so on, or they may provide each of those bundled with WordPress, MediaWiki, MariaDB, or another popular software package.

In the case of our generic cloud provider, a list of images can be returned simply by requesting the `images` resource:

```
def avail_images():
    '''
    Get list of available VM images
    '''
    return _query(resource='images')
```

In a profile configuration, an image is specified using the `image` argument.

Listing sizes

Sizes are a concept that is unique to cloud providers, and indeed not every cloud provider even supports them. Depending on the provider, size usually refers to a combination of the number of processors, processor speed, amount of RAM, disk space, type of disk (platter versus SSD), and so on.

Once again, our generic cloud provider will return a list of sizes under the `sizes` resource:

```
def avail_sizes():
    '''
    Get list of available VM sizes
    '''
    return _query(resource='sizes')
```

In a profile configuration, a size is specified using the `size` argument.

Listing locations

Depending on the cloud provider, a location may refer to a specific data center, a region in some part of the world, or even a specific data center inside a region that contains multiple data centers.

As we said before, the location is often prepended to the URL used to talk to the API. In the case of our generic cloud provider, locations are queried using the `regions` resource.

```
def avail_locations():
    '''
    Get list of available locations
    '''
    return _query(resource='locations')
```

In a profile configuration, a location is specified using the `location` argument.

Listing nodes

The next thing to do is display the nodes that currently exist inside the account for that cloud provider. There are three `salt-cloud` arguments to display node data: `-Q` or `--query`, `-F` or `--full-query`, and `-S` or `--select-query`. Each of these options will query every configured cloud provider, and return all of the information at once.

Querying standard node data

There are six pieces of information that should always be provided for each node. This data is displayed when the `-Q` argument is used with `salt-cloud`:

- `id`: The ID of this VM, as used by the cloud provider.
- `image`: The image used to create this VM. If this data is not available, it should be set to `None`.
- `size`: The size used to create this VM. If this data is not available, it should be set to `None`.
- `state`: The current running state of this VM. This is usually `RUNNING`, `STOPPED`, `PENDING` (the VM is still booting), or `TERMINATED` (the VM has been destroyed, but not yet cleaned up). If this data is not available, it should be set to None.
- `private_ips`: Any private IP addresses that are used on a cloud provider's internal network. These should be returned as a list. If this data is not available, the list should be empty.
- `public_ips`: Any public IP addresses that are available for this VM. Any IPv6 addresses should be included here. These IPs should be returned as a list. If this data is not available, the list should be empty.

Users should have access to all of these variables, even if they are empty or set to None. This is also the only data that should be returned by the -Q argument. To return this data, we use a function called `list_nodes()`:

```
def list_nodes():
    '''
    List of nodes, with standard query data
    '''
    ret = {}
    nodes = _query(resource='instances')
    for node in nodes:
        ret[node] = {
            'id': nodes[node]['id'],
            'image': nodes[node].get('image', None),
            'size': nodes[node].get('size', None),
            'state': nodes[node].get('state', None),
            'private_ips': nodes[node].get('private_ips', []),
            'public_ips': nodes[node].get('public_ips', []),
        }
    return ret
```

Querying full node data

VMs usually contain quite a bit more information than is returned with -Q. If you want to view all of the information that a cloud provider is willing and able to display to you, you use the -F flag. This corresponds to a function called `list_nodes_full()`:

```
def list_nodes_full():
    '''
    List of nodes, with full node data
    '''
    return _query(resource='instances')
```

Sometimes, you are only interested in a very specific set of data. For instance, you may only want to display a VM's ID, public IPs, and state. The -S option allows you to perform a query that returns only a selection of the fields that are available with a full query. The selection itself is defined as a list in the main cloud configuration file (usually /etc/salt/cloud):

```
query.selection:
  - id
  - public_ips
  - state
```

The query itself is performed by a function called `list_nodes_select()`. Some providers may require something special to be done to separate out this data, but most of the time you can just use the `list_nodes_select()` function that ships with the `salt.utils.cloud` library:

```
import salt.utils.cloud


def list_nodes_select():
    '''
    Return a list of the VMs that are on the provider, with select
    fields
    '''
    return salt.utils.cloud.list_nodes_select(
        list_nodes_full('function'), __opts__['query.selection'],
    )
```

Creating a VM

The most complex part of any cloud module has traditionally been the `create()` function. That's because this function doesn't just spin up a VM. Its tasks can generally be split up into these components:

- Request that the cloud provider create a VM
- Wait for that VM to become available
- Log in to that VM and install Salt
- Accept that's VM's Minion keys on the Master

Some more complex cloud providers may include additional steps, such as requesting different types of VMs based on the profile configuration, or attaching volumes to the VM. In addition, the `create()` function should fire events along Salt's event bus, to let the Master know how far along it is with the creation process.

Before we get into the `create()` function, we should put together another function called `request_instance()`. This function will do two things for us:

- It can be called directly from `create()`, which will simplify the `create()` function
- It can be called outside of `create()`, when a non-Salt VM is needed

This function doesn't need to do much. As the name implies, it need only request that the cloud provider create a VM. But it will need to collect together some information to build the HTTP request:

```python
def request_instance(vm_):
    '''
    Request that a VM be created
    '''
    request_kwargs = {
        'name': vm_['name'],
        'image': vm_['image'],
        'size': vm_['size'],
        'location': vm_['location']
    }

    salt.utils.cloud.fire_event(
        'event',
        'requesting instance',
        'salt/cloud/{0}/requesting'.format(vm_['name']),
        {'kwargs': request_kwargs},
        transport=__opts__['transport']
    )

    return _query(
        resource='instances',
        method='POST',
        data=request_kwargs,
    )
```

You've probably noticed the call to `salt.utils.cloud.fire_event()` in this function. Every time you do something major in the `create()` function (or in functions that are called by `create()`), you should fire an event that gives some information about what you're about to do. Those events will be picked up by the event reactor, allowing the Master to keep track of progress and perform additional tasks if configured to do so, at the right time.

We're also going to create a function called `query_instance()`. This function will watch a newly requested VM, and wait for an IP address to become available. This IP address will be used to log in to the VM and provision it.

```python
def query_instance(vm_):
    '''
    Query a VM upon creation
    '''
    salt.utils.cloud.fire_event(
```

```
            'event',
            'querying instance',
            'salt/cloud/{0}/querying'.format(vm_['name']),
            transport=__opts__['transport']
        )


    def _query_ip_address():
        nodes = list_nodes_full()
        data = nodes.get(vm_['name'], None)
        if not data:
            return False

        if 'public_ips' in data:
            return data['public_ips']
        return None

    data = salt.utils.cloud.wait_for_ip(
        _query_ip_address,
        timeout=config.get_cloud_config_value(
            'wait_for_ip_timeout', vm_, __opts__, default=10 *
            60),
        interval=config.get_cloud_config_value(
            'wait_for_ip_interval', vm_, __opts__, default=10),
        interval_multiplier=config.get_cloud_config_value(
            'wait_for_ip_interval_multiplier', vm_, __opts__,
            default=1),
    )


    return data
```

This function makes use of another function that ships with Salt called `salt.utils.
cloud.wait_for_ip()`. That function takes a callback, which we're defining as a
nested function called `_query_ip_address()`. That nested function checks to see if
an IP address exists. If it does, then `salt.utils.cloud.wait_for_ip()` will stop
waiting and move on. If it does not yet exist, then it will keep waiting.

There are three more arguments that we're passing in as well. `timeout` defines how
long to wait for an IP address to show up at all (in our case, ten minutes); `interval`
tells Salt Cloud how long to wait between queries (our default is ten seconds).

You may be tempted to use a much shorter interval, but many cloud providers
will throttle requests if an account seems to be abusing its privileges. On that note,
`interval_multiplier` will increase `interval` after each request. For instance, if
`interval` was set to 1 and `interval_multiplier` was set to 2, then requests would
be spaced out at 1 second, then 2, 4, 8, 16, 32, and so on.

With those two functions in place, we can finally set up our `create()` function. It requires one argument, which is a dictionary containing a combination of the profile, provider, and main cloud configuration data:

```
def create(vm_):
    '''
    Create a single VM
    '''
    salt.utils.cloud.fire_event(
        'event',
        'starting create',
        'salt/cloud/{0}/creating'.format(vm_['name']),
        {
            'name': vm_['name'],
            'profile': vm_['profile'],
            'provider': vm_['driver'],
        },
        transport=__opts__['transport']
    )

    create_data = request_instance(vm_)
    query_data = query_instance(vm_)

    vm_['key_filename'] = config.get_cloud_config_value(
        'private_key', vm_, __opts__, search_global=False,
        default=None
    )
    vm_['ssh_host'] = query_data['public_ips'][0]

    salt.utils.cloud.bootstrap(vm_, __opts__)

    salt.utils.cloud.fire_event(
        'event',
        'created instance',
        'salt/cloud/{0}/created'.format(vm_['name']),
        {
            'name': vm_['name'],
            'profile': vm_['profile'],
            'provider': vm_['driver'],
        },
        transport=__opts__['transport']
    )

    return query_data
```

We begin our function by firing an event stating that a creation process is being started. We then allow `request_instance()` and `query_instance()` to do their work, pull the name of an SSH key filename from the profile data, and then scrape an IP address to use to log in to the box from the VM data.

The next step involves waiting for the VM to become available, and then logging in and provisioning it. But since that part of the process is the same across cloud providers, it's all been rolled into another helper function inside `salt.utils.cloud` called `bootstrap()`. The `bootstrap()` function will even fire additional events for us, keeping the event reactor apprised of its own status.

When all is said and done, we fire one last event stating the information about the VM, and return the VM's data to the user.

You may have noticed that the events that we fire all include a tag starting with `salt/cloud/`, then the VM's name, then a short name for the step that we are currently performing. If you are working with a more complex cloud provider and wish to fire other events that are specific to them, keep the tag looking the same way, with as simple a descriptor as possible. This will help your users keep track of all of your cloud tags.

Destroying VMs

It's just as important to be able to destroy a VM as it is to be able to create one, but the process is thankfully much easier. Keep in mind that events should also be fired when destroying: once before it happens, and once after:

```
def destroy(name):
    '''
    Destroy a machine by name
    '''
    salt.utils.cloud.fire_event(
        'event',
        'destroying instance',
        'salt/cloud/{0}/destroying'.format(name),
        {'name': name},
        transport=__opts__['transport']
    )

    nodes = list_nodes_full()
    ret = _query(
        resource='instances/{0}'.format(nodes[name]['id']),
        location=node['location'],
```

```
        method='DELETE'
    )

    salt.utils.cloud.fire_event(
        'event',
        'destroyed instance',
        'salt/cloud/{0}/destroyed'.format(name),
        {'name': name},
        transport=__opts__['transport']
    )

    if __opts__.get('update_cachedir', False) is True:
        salt.utils.cloud.delete_minion_cachedir(
            name, __active_provider_name__.split(':')[0], __opts__
        )

    return ret
```

We've done one more important thing in this function. Salt Cloud has the ability to maintain a cache of information about VMs. We didn't see this before, because the bootstrap() function handles populating the cache when a VM is created. However, since there is no generic method for destroying machines, we need to handle this manually.

Using actions and functions

So far, all of the functions that we've written are called directly using a special command-line argument (such as --query or --provision). However, there are other operations that cloud providers may be able to perform that are not necessarily as standard as the ones that we've seen so far.

For instance, most cloud providers have API methods for start, stop, and restart. But some providers don't support all of those; start and stop may be available, but not restart. Or start and restart, but not stop. Other operations, such as listing SSH keys, may be available on one cloud provider, but not another.

When it comes down to it, there are two types of operations that can be performed against a cloud provider. Operations that are specific to a VM (stop, start, restart, and so on) are known in Salt Cloud as **actions**. Operations that interact with a component of the cloud provider, that are not specific to a VM (listing SSH keys, modifying users, and so on), are known in Salt Cloud as **functions**.

Using actions

Actions are called using the `--action` argument with the `salt-cloud` command. Because they operate on a specific VM, the first argument passed to them is a name. If other arguments are passed in from the command line, they will show up in a dictionary called `kwargs`. There is one more argument, called `call`, which tells a function whether it was called with `--action` or `--function`. You can use this to inform users when they have called an action or function incorrectly:

```
def rename(name, kwargs, call=None):
    '''
    Properly rename a node. Pass in the new name as "newname".
    '''
    if call != 'action':
        raise SaltCloudSystemExit(
            'The rename action must be called with -a or --
            action.'
        )

    salt.utils.cloud.rename_key(
        __opts__['pki_dir'], name, kwargs['newname']
    )

    nodes = list_nodes_full()
    return _query(
        resource='instances/{0}'.format(nodes[name]['id']),
        action='rename',
        method='POST',
        data={'name': kwargs['newname']}
    )
```

Even if you do not plan to issue a warning to users, you must accept the `call` argument; it will be passed to it regardless, and an error will be raised if it isn't there.

Once again, I've sprung another surprise on you. Since this action will be renaming a VM, we need to notify Salt as well. If we don't, then the Master will be unable to contact the Minion. As usual, there is a helper function (`salt.utils.cloud.rename_key()`) that does the work for us.

Using functions

Because functions do not operate on a specific VM, they do not require a name argument. However, they do require the `kwargs` and `call` arguments, even if you don't intend to use them for anything.

```
def show_image(kwargs, call=None):
    '''
    Show the details for a VM image
    '''
    if call != 'function':
        raise SaltCloudSystemExit(
            'The show_image function must be called with -f or --
            function.'
        )

    return _query(resource='images/{0}'.format(kwargs['image']))
```

If you add the call argument to various functions throughout your module, you will be able to call them directly using the `--action` or `--function` arguments. This can be very useful for, say, the `list_nodes()` functions, when you want to look at VMs for only one cloud provider at a time, rather than all of them at once.

The only public function that cannot be called this way is the `create()` function. `destroy()` can be called using the `--action` argument, and almost everything else that we've added so far can be called using the `--function` argument. We'll go ahead and add those in for our final cloud module.

The final cloud module

When we have finished, the final cloud module will look like this:

```
'''
Generic Salt Cloud module

This module is not designed for any specific cloud provider, but is generic
enough that only minimal changes may be required for some providers.

This file should be saved as salt/cloud/clouds/generic.py

Set up the cloud configuration at ``/etc/salt/cloud.providers`` or
``/etc/salt/cloud.providers.d/generic.conf``:
```

```
.. code-block:: yaml

    my-cloud-config:
        driver: generic
        # The login user
        user: larry
        # The user's password
        password: 123pass
'''
import json
import salt.utils.http
import salt.utils.cloud
import salt.config as config
from salt.exceptions import SaltCloudSystemExit


__virtualname__ = 'generic'


def __virtual__():
    '''
    Check for cloud configs
    '''
    if get_configured_provider() is False:
        return False

    return __virtualname__


def get_configured_provider():
    '''
    Make sure configuration is correct
    '''
    return config.is_provider_configured(
        __opts__,
        __active_provider_name__ or __virtualname__,
        ('user', 'password')
    )


def request_instance(vm_):
    '''
    Request that a VM be created
    '''
```

```
        request_kwargs = {
            'name': vm_['name'],
            'image': vm_['image'],
            'size': vm_['size'],
            'location': vm_['location']
        }

        salt.utils.cloud.fire_event(
            'event',
            'requesting instance',
            'salt/cloud/{0}/requesting'.format(vm_['name']),
            {'kwargs': request_kwargs},
            transport=__opts__['transport']
        )

        return _query(
            resource='instances',
            method='POST',
            data=request_kwargs,
        )


def query_instance(vm_):
    '''
    Query a VM upon creation
    '''
    salt.utils.cloud.fire_event(
        'event',
        'querying instance',
        'salt/cloud/{0}/querying'.format(vm_['name']),
        transport=__opts__['transport']
    )

    def _query_ip_address():
        nodes = list_nodes_full()
        data = nodes.get(vm_['name'], None)
        if not data:
            log.error('There was an empty response from the cloud
            provider')
            return False

        log.debug('Returned query data: {0}'.format(data))
```

```
            if 'public_ips' in data:
                return data['public_ips']
            return None

        data = salt.utils.cloud.wait_for_ip(
            _query_ip_address,
            timeout=config.get_cloud_config_value(
                'wait_for_ip_timeout', vm_, __opts__, default=10 *
                60),
            interval=config.get_cloud_config_value(
                'wait_for_ip_interval', vm_, __opts__, default=10),
            interval_multiplier=config.get_cloud_config_value(
                'wait_for_ip_interval_multiplier', vm_, __opts__,
                default=1),
        )

        return data


def create(vm_):
    '''
    Create a single VM
    '''
    salt.utils.cloud.fire_event(
        'event',
        'starting create',
        'salt/cloud/{0}/creating'.format(vm_['name']),
        {
            'name': vm_['name'],
            'profile': vm_['profile'],
            'provider': vm_['driver'],
        },
        transport=__opts__['transport']
    )

    create_data = request_instance(vm_)
    query_data = query_instance(vm_)

    vm_['key_filename'] = config.get_cloud_config_value(
        'private_key', vm_, __opts__, search_global=False,
        default=None
    )
    vm_['ssh_host'] = query_data['public_ips'][0]
```

```
        salt.utils.cloud.bootstrap(vm_, __opts__)

        salt.utils.cloud.fire_event(
            'event',
            'created instance',
            'salt/cloud/{0}/created'.format(vm_['name']),
            {
                'name': vm_['name'],
                'profile': vm_['profile'],
                'provider': vm_['driver'],
            },
            transport=__opts__['transport']
        )

        return query_data


    def destroy(name, call=None):
        '''
        Destroy a machine by name
        '''
        salt.utils.cloud.fire_event(
            'event',
            'destroying instance',
            'salt/cloud/{0}/destroying'.format(name),
            {'name': name},
            transport=__opts__['transport']
        )

        nodes = list_nodes_full()
        ret = _query(
            resource='instances/{0}'.format(nodes[name]['id']),
            location=node['location'],
            method='DELETE'
        )

        salt.utils.cloud.fire_event(
            'event',
            'destroyed instance',
            'salt/cloud/{0}/destroyed'.format(name),
            {'name': name},
            transport=__opts__['transport']
        )
```

```
        if __opts__.get('update_cachedir', False) is True:
            salt.utils.cloud.delete_minion_cachedir(
                name, __active_provider_name__.split(':')[0], __opts__
            )

        return ret


def rename(name, kwargs, call=None):
    '''
    Properly rename a node. Pass in the new name as "newname".
    '''
    if call != 'action':
        raise SaltCloudSystemExit(
            'The rename action must be called with -a or --
            action.'
        )

    salt.utils.cloud.rename_key(
        __opts__['pki_dir'], name, kwargs['newname']
    )

    nodes = list_nodes_full()
    return _query(
        resource='instances/{0}'.format(nodes[name]['id']),
        action='rename',
        method='POST',
        data={'name': kwargs['newname']}
    )


def show_image(kwargs, call=None):
    '''
    Show the details for a VM image
    '''
    if call != 'function':
        raise SaltCloudSystemExit(
            'The show_image function must be called with -f or --
            function.'
        )

    return _query(resource='images/{0}'.format(kwargs['image']))
```

```
def list_nodes(call=None):
    '''
    List of nodes, with standard query data
    '''
    ret = {}
    nodes = _query(resource='instances')
    for node in nodes:
        ret[node] = {
            'id': nodes[node]['id'],
            'image': nodes[node].get('image', None),
            'size': nodes[node].get('size', None),
            'state': nodes[node].get('state', None),
            'private_ips': nodes[node].get('private_ips', []),
            'public_ips': nodes[node].get('public_ips', []),
        }
    return ret


def list_nodes_full(call=None):
    '''
    List of nodes, with full node data
    '''
    return _query(resource='instances')


def list_nodes_select(call=None):
    '''
    Return a list of the VMs that are on the provider, with select
    fields
    '''
    return salt.utils.cloud.list_nodes_select(
        list_nodes_full('function'), __opts__['query.selection'],
        call,
    )


def avail_images(call=None):
    '''
    Get list of available VM images
    '''
    return _query(resource='images')
```

```
def avail_sizes(call=None):
    '''
    Get list of available VM sizes
    '''
    return _query(resource='sizes')


def avail_locations(call=None):
    '''
    Get list of available locations
    '''
    return _query(resource='locations')


def _query(
        resource=None,
        action=None,
        params=None,
        method='GET',
        location=None,
        data=None
):
    '''
    Make a web call to the cloud provider
    '''
    user = config.get_cloud_config_value(
        'user', get_configured_provider(), __opts__,
        search_global=False
    )
    password = config.get_cloud_config_value(
        'password', get_configured_provider(), __opts__,
    )
    api_key = config.get_cloud_config_value(
        'api_key', get_configured_provider(), __opts__,
    )
    location = config.get_cloud_config_value(
        'location', get_configured_provider(), __opts__,
        default=None
    )

    if location is None:
        location = 'eu-north'
```

```
url = 'https://{0}.api.example.com/v1'.format(location)

if resource:
    url += '/{0}'.format(resource)

if action:
    url += '/{0}'.format(action)

if not isinstance(params, dict):
    params = {}

params['api_key'] = api_key

if data is not None:
    data = json.dumps(data)

result = salt.utils.http.query(
    url,
    method,
    params=params,
    data=data,
    decode=True,
    decode_type='json',
    hide_fields=['api_key'],
    opts=__opts__,
)

return result['dict']
```

Troubleshooting cloud modules

Cloud modules may seem daunting because there are so many components that are required to make a cohesive piece of code. But if you work on the module with bite-sized chunks, it will be a lot easier to handle.

Write avail_sizes() or avail_images() first

Whenever I write a new cloud module, the first thing I do is get some sample code working that makes a small query. Because images and sizes are critical to the creation of a VM, and because those calls tend to be very simple, they are usually the easiest to get working.

Once you have one of those functions working, break it out into a _query() function (if you didn't start that way) and a function that calls it. Then write another function that calls it. You may find yourself tweaking _query() for each of the first few functions, but then it will stabilize and require few, if any, changes.

Use shortcuts

I cannot tell you how many hours I have spent waiting for VMs to spin up, just to test one piece of code. If you break out the create() function into a lot of smaller functions, then you can temporarily hardcode VM data as needed, and skip over operations that would otherwise waste too much time. Just be sure to take out the shortcuts when you finish!

Summary

Salt Cloud is designed to handle compute resources, though additional cloud functionality can be added as needed. A cloud module can be written using Libcloud, an SDK, or the direct REST API; each method has its pros and cons. Modern REST APIs tend to be very similar and easy to work with. There are several functions that are required for a cohesive cloud module, but most are not complex. Actions are performed against individual VMs while functions are performed against cloud providers themselves.

Now that we've gone over cloud modules, it's time to start monitoring our resources. Next up: beacons.

10
Monitoring with Beacons

Beacons are a newer type of module in Salt which are designed to watch resources on a Minion, and report to the Master when those resources fall out of alignment with what you expect them to look like. In this chapter, we will discuss:

- Monitoring external systems with Salt
- Troubleshooting beacons

Watching for data

There are two basic types of monitoring services: those that record data, and those that trigger alerts based on that data. On the surface, beacons may look like the second type. They run on a regular interval (as frequently as every second, by default) and when they find data that is important, they send it up to the Master.

However, because beacons have access to execution modules on the Minion that they are running on, they can interact with any program on the Minion that an execution module can.

Keeping an eye on things

Let's go ahead and put together a beacon that monitors `nspawn` containers. It doesn't need to be very complex; indeed, beacons should be as simple as possible, since they are expected to run so often. All that our beacon needs to do is keep an eye on containers that should be running, and those that should be absent.

Containers have become very popular in the modern data center, thanks in large part to Docker and LXC. systemd has its own containering system called nspawn, which is a very powerful system in its own right. A number of Linux distributions now ship with systemd, which means that you may already have nspawn installed. You can find a more complete discussion of nspawn itself on Lennart Pottering's blog at:

`http://0pointer.net/blog/systemd-for-administrators-part-xxi.html`

First, we need to set up our __virtual__() function. Since nspawn is part of systemd, and not every Minion will have systemd on it, we need to perform a check for it. However, since we're going to use the nspawn execution module that ships with Salt, and it already contains a __virtual__() function, all that we really need to do is make sure it is present:

```
'''
Send events covering nspawn containers

This beacon accepts a list of containers and whether they should be
running or absent:

beacons:
  nspawn:
    vsftpd: absent
    httpd: running

This file should be saved as salt/beacons/nspawn.py
'''
__virtualname__ = 'nspawn'


def __virtual__():
    '''
    Ensure that systemd-nspawn is available
    '''
    if 'nspawn.list_running' in __salt__:
        return __virtualname__
    return False
```

It makes sense to check specifically for nspawn.list_running, since that is the only function that we'll be using here.

Validating configuration

Beacons will not run unless they know which data to watch for. You probably saw the configuration example in the preceding docstring. The `validate()` function checks the configuration that was passed to this beacon, to make sure that it has been formatted in the correct way.

If we were going to be minimalistic about this, then we would just check to make sure that the correct type of data has been passed in. In our case, we're expecting a dictionary, so we could get away with just checking for that:

```
def validate(config):
    '''
    Validate the beacon configuration
    '''
    if not isinstance(config, dict):
        return False
    return True
```

But we'll go ahead and add just a little more, to make sure that, at the very least, the containers listed are set to one of the required values: running or absent:

```
def validate(config):
    '''
    Validate the beacon configuration
    '''
    if not isinstance(config, dict):
        return False
    for key in config:
        if config[key] not in ('running', 'absent'):
            return False
    return True
```

You can skip this function if you need to; if it's not there, then Salt will skip over it. However, it is a good idea to have it there, to help keep bad configuration from causing the beacon to crash with a stacktrace.

The beacon() function

As with some of the other types of modules, beacons have a function that is required, since Salt will look for it when trying to use the module. Not surprisingly, this function is called `beacon()`. It is passed the same `config` data as the `validate()` function.

Our beacon's only job is to use `machinectl` to report which containers are currently running on the Minion. Its output looks something like the following:

```
# machinectl list
MACHINE         CLASS       SERVICE
vsftpd          container systemd-nspawn


1 machines listed.
```

We could call this manually and parse the output ourselves, but as I said before, there is already an `nspawn` execution module that ships with Salt, and it has a `list_running()` function that does all of that for us.

All that we have to do then is get a list of the nodes that are reported as running, and then match it against the list of nodes in the `config` dictionary:

```
def beacon(config):
    '''
    Scan for nspawn containers and fire events
    '''
    nodes = __salt__['nspawn.list_running']()
    ret = []
    for name in config:
        if config[name] == 'running':
            if name not in nodes:
                ret.append({name: 'Absent'})
        elif config[name] == 'absent':
            if name in nodes:
                ret.append({name: 'Running'})
        else:
            if name not in nodes:
                ret.append({name: False})

    return ret
```

Rather than stepping through the list of running nodes, we iterate through the list of nodes that were configured. If a node that should be absent shows up in the running list, then we mark it as running. If it should be running but doesn't show up, then we mark it as absent.

That last `else` statement will notify us if something that wasn't marked as running or absent showed up in the list. Since we already did that check in the `validate()` function, this shouldn't be needed. But it's not a bad idea to keep this kind of check in there, just in case your `validate()` function missed something. If you start seeing events from this module that have nodes set to `False`, then you know you need to go back and check the `validate()` function.

If you've been following along and have already started testing this module, then you may notice something, well, obnoxious. By default, beacons are executed once a second. You can change that interval on a per-module basis:

```
beacons:
  nspawn:
    vsftpd: present
    httpd: absent
    interval: 30
```

With that configuration, the `nspawn` beacon will only be executed once every five seconds, instead of every second. That will cut down on the chatter, but also means that your beacon won't necessarily be watching as often as you'd like.

Let's go ahead and add some code, which will allow the beacon to run as often as you'd like, but send updates on a less regular basis. Let's say that you have your beacon tied into a monitoring service (through the event reactor), and you want up-to-the-second monitoring, but you don't need to be told more than once every five minutes that, "oh, by the way, the container is still down":

```python
import time
def beacon(config):
    '''
    Scan for nspawn containers and fire events
    '''
    interval = __salt__['config.get']('nspawn_alert_interval',
    360)
    now = int(time.time())

    nodes = __salt__['nspawn.list_running']()
    ret = []
    for name in config:
        lasttime = __grains__.get('nspawn_last_notify',
        {}).get(name, 0)
        if config[name] == 'running':
            if name not in nodes:
                if now - lasttime >= interval:
                    ret.append({name: 'Absent'})
```

```
                        __salt__['grains.setval']('nspawn_last_notify',
{name: now})
            elif config[name] == 'absent':
                if name in nodes:
                    if now - lasttime >= interval:
                        ret.append({name: 'Running'})
                        __salt__['grains.setval']('nspawn_last_notify',
{name: now})
            else:
                if name not in nodes:
                    if now - lasttime >= interval:
                        ret.append({name: False})
                            __salt__['grains.setval']('nspawn_last_
notify', {name: now})

        return ret
```

First, we set up an alert interval called `nspawn_alert_interval`, and default it to `360` seconds (or, every five minutes). Because we used `config.get` to look for it, we can configure it in either the `master` or `minion` configuration files, or in a grain or a pillar for the Minion.

Then we make a note of the current time using Python's own `time.time()` function. This function reports the number of seconds since the epoch, which is perfect for our purposes, since our alert interval is also configured in seconds.

As we iterate through the list of configured nodes, we check to see when the last notification was sent out. This is stored in a grain called `nspawn_last_notify`. This isn't a grain that your users will be updating; this is one that the beacon will keep track of.

In fact, you will see that happen for each of the branches in the `if` statement. Whenever the beacon detects that an alert should be sent, it first checks to see if an alert has already been sent during the specified interval. If not, then it sets up an event to be returned.

Watching for beacons

Beacons use Salt's event bus to send notifications to the Master. You can use the `event` function in the `state` runner to watch the beacons come in on the event bus. The return from this particular beacon module will look like the following:

```
salt/beacon/alton/nspawn/        {
    "_stamp": "2016-01-17T17:48:48.986662",
    "data": {
```

```
            "vsftpd": "Present",
            "id": "alton"
        },
        "tag": "salt/beacon/alton/nspawn/"
    }
```

Take note of the tag, which contains salt/beacon/, followed by the ID of the Minion (alton) that fired the beacon, and then the name of the beacon itself (nspawn).

The final beacon module

When all is said and done, our final beacon module will look like this:

```
    '''
    Send events covering nspawn containers

    This beacon accepts a list of containers and whether they should be
    running or absent:

        .. code-block:: yaml

            beacons:
              nspawn:
                vsftpd: running
                httpd: absent


    This file should be saved as salt/beacons/nspawn.py
    '''
    import time


    __virtualname__ = 'nspawn'


    def __virtual__():
        '''
        Ensure that systemd-nspawn is available
        '''
        if 'nspawn.list_running' in __salt__:
            return __virtualname__
        return False
```

```python
def validate(config):
    '''
    Validate the beacon configuration
    '''
    if not isinstance(config, dict):
        return False
    for key in config:
        if config[key] not in ('running', 'absent'):
            return False
    return True


def beacon(config):
    '''
    Scan for nspawn containers and fire events
    '''
    interval = __salt__['config.get']('nspawn_alert_interval',
    360)
    now = int(time.time())

    nodes = __salt__['nspawn.list_running']()
    ret = []
    for name in config:
        lasttime = __grains__.get('nspawn_last_notify',
        {}).get(name, 0)
        if config[name] == 'running':
            if name not in nodes:
                if now - lasttime >= interval:
                    ret.append({name: 'Absent'})
                    __salt__['grains.setval']('nspawn_last_notify',
{name: now})
        elif config[name] == 'absent':
            if name in nodes:
                if now - lasttime >= interval:
                    ret.append({name: 'Running'})
                    __salt__['grains.setval']('nspawn_last_notify',
{name: now})
        else:
            if name not in nodes:
                if now - lasttime >= interval:
                    ret.append({name: False})
                    __salt__['grains.setval']('nspawn_last_notify',
{name: now})

    return ret
```

Troubleshooting beacons

Beacons are a type of module that require both a running Master and a running Minion. Running the `salt-master` service in the foreground won't give you much insight, since the code will be running on the Minion, but running the `salt-minion` service in the foreground will be very helpful:

```
# salt-minion -l debug
```

Set aside a Minion that only has your beacon configured and no others. By default, these beacons will run every second, and that can generate very noisy logs indeed:

```
[INFO    ] Executing command 'machinectl --no-legend --no-pager list' in
directory '/root'
[DEBUG   ] stdout: vsftpd container systemd-nspawn
[INFO    ] Executing command 'machinectl --no-legend --no-pager list' in
directory '/root'
[DEBUG   ] stdout: vsftpd container systemd-nspawn
[INFO    ] Executing command 'machinectl --no-legend --no-pager list' in
directory '/root'
[DEBUG   ] stdout: vsftpd container systemd-nspawn
```

Imagine several beacons running at once, each logging its own data for what it's currently doing. That will get old fast.

You will also want to keep an event listener open on the Master:

```
# salt-run state.event pretty=True

    salt/beacon/alton/nspawn/        {
        "_stamp": "2016-01-17T17:48:48.986662",
        "data": {
            "ftp-container": "Present",
            "id": "alton"
        },
        "tag": "salt/beacon/alton/nspawn/"
    }
```

Fortunately, beacons are not the sort of thing that you really need to wait around for; just make the machine exhibit the kind of behavior that you're looking for, and then start up the `salt-minion` process. Just make sure to test for any variation of the behavior that you expect to find, whether or not it is expected to return an event.

Summary

Beacons give Minions the ability to raise events based on monitored conditions. A validate() function is helpful for ensuring that the configuration is correct, but it is not required. A beacon() function is required, as it is the function that performs the actual monitoring. Use execution modules when possible to perform the heavy lifting. Beacons can run at very short intervals, but by having them store data in grains, you can set notifications at longer intervals.

Now that we have all of the Minion-side modules in the book out of the way, let's go back and finish up with some Master-side modules. Next up: extending the Master.

11
Extending the Master

Even though some of the modules that we've written so far can be used on the Master, the focus has still been entirely on managing Minion-based operations. Even runners, which only run on the Master, were originally designed to script tasks between Minions.

There are two types of modules that are designed entirely for Master-side work: external authentication modules and wheel modules. In this chapter, we'll go over:

- Adding external authentication to the Master
- Troubleshooting external authentication modules
- Managing Master configuration with wheel modules
- Troubleshooting wheel modules

Using external authentication

In its default setup, users only communicate with Salt with one user: usually either `root` or `salt`. Any user who has access to log in as that user will be able to issue Salt commands. This may be OK with smaller setups, but it does not scale well at all. Larger organizations will want each user to manage Salt with their own login, and be able to set access controls on a per-user basis. There are also other programs, including Salt API, which require the use of external authentication modules.

External authentication (or **auth or eauth**) modules allow individual users to have their own permissions to the various components of Salt. The simplest is probably the `pam` module, in part because other existing access control mechanisms can be configured inside PAM itself. Unfortunately, PAM is rarely used outside of Linux, so other modules are needed on other platforms.

Authenticating credentials

On the surface, an auth module doesn't need to do much. It only needs to accept a username and password, and check with the appropriate service to ensure that it is valid. If it is, then it returns `True`. Otherwise, it will return `False`.

Let's go ahead and set up an auth module for a fictional web service that accepts a username and password, and returns a status of `200` (`OK`) if they are correct and `403` (`FORBIDDEN`) if they are not. As with some of the other module types, there is a required function in auth modules. This one is called `auth()`. Let's go ahead and look at our entire auth module at once:

```
'''
Provide authentication using an authentication web service. This service
must be configured with an API ID and API key in the master
configuration.

webauth:
  apiid: 0123456789
  apikey: abcdef0123456789abcdef0123456789

This file should be saved as salt/auth/webauth.py
'''
import json
import base64
import urllib
import salt.utils.http


def auth(username, password):
    '''
    Authenticate using an external web authentication service
    '''
    apiid = __opts__.get('webauth', {}).get('apiid', None)
    apikey = __opts__.get('webauth', {}).get('apikey', None)
    url = 'https://api.example.com/v1/checkauth'

    username = urllib.quote(username)
    password = urllib.quote(password)
    data = {
        'type': 'basic',
```

```
        'value': base64.b64encode('{0}:{1}'.format(username,
        password))
    }

    result = salt.utils.http.query(
        path,
        method='POST',
        username=apiid,
        password=apikey,
        data=json.dumps(data),
        status=True,
        opts=__opts__,
    )
    if result.get('status', 403) == 200:
        return True

    return False
```

Our function declaration has two required arguments: username and password.
These will be sent to the authentication service to check their validity. Our service
doesn't just accept arbitrary credentials; it requires an account to be set up first,
with its own authentication, which stores the username and password. So, our first
job is to grab the credentials for that service (apiid and apikey) from the master
configuration. Then add in the URL to be used for the authentication check:

```
apiid = __opts__.get('webauth', {}).get('apiid', None)
apikey = __opts__.get('webauth', {}).get('apikey', None)
url = 'https://api.example.com/v1/checkauth'
```

We want to be able to accept special characters in either the username or password,
but since they won't translate properly over the wire, we use Python's urllib library
to add quoting to them. Then we format the credentials in the way that the external
web service expects:

```
username = urllib.quote(username)
password = urllib.quote(password)
data = {
    'type': 'basic',
    'value': base64.b64encode('{0}:{1}'.format(username,
    password))
}
```

Now that we have all of the data set up to pass to the web service, we use the `http.query()` function to make the call. `apiid` and `apikey` are used as the username and password to the service itself, and the user's username and password are set along as a JSON string. We also make sure to tell `http.query()` to return a status code, since that is the only part of the result that we care about:

```
result = salt.utils.http.query(
    path,
    method='POST',
    username=apiid,
    password=apikey,
    data=json.dumps(data),
    status=True,
    opts=__opts__,
)
```

Once we have an authentication code, we check to see if it's `200`. If something goes wrong and there is no code, then we default the value to `403`, but when it comes down to it, anything other than `200` means that the credentials will be considered invalid:

```
if result.get('status', 403) == 200:
    return True

return False
```

Troubleshooting external authentication

Troubleshooting `auth` modules is a little different from other types of module, because what you're testing is the ability to access a command, not the functionality of the resulting command. This means that the command that you choose to execute should be one that is already known to work, such as `test.ping`.

Setting auth parameters

Before you can use an `auth` module, you need to enable it in the master configuration file. Multiple auth modules can be configured, using the `external_auth` directive:

```
external_auth:
  pam:
    moe:
      - .*
      - '@runner'
      - '@wheel'
```

```
    larry:
        - test.*
        - disk.*
        - network.*
        - '@runner'
        - '@wheel'
  webauth:
    shemp:
        - test.*
        - network.*
        - '@runner'
        - '@wheel'
```

In this example, we have three users set, between two different `auth` modules. The `moe` and `larry` users are set to use the `pam` module, and the `shemp` user is set to use the `webauth` module that we just created. The `moe` user has access to all execution modules, plus the runner and wheel systems, while `larry`'s execution module access is limited to the `test`, `disk`, and `network` modules. The `shemp` user is the same as `larry`, minus access to the `disk` module.

Keep in mind that Salt API requires `@runner` and `@wheel` to be set. If you are not planning on giving users access to resources using Salt API, then you can skip those two lines.

Once you have `external_auth` configured, there are two means of testing `auth` modules: using the `salt` command on the Master, and using Salt API.

Testing with the salt command

The fastest way to test an `auth` module is to log in to the Master with the account that the `salt-master` service is running as and issue a `salt` command, with the appropriate arguments to set which `auth` module is to be used, and which credentials to use:

- `--auth` or `-a`: This argument sets which auth module to use. The default argument for this is `pam`.

- `--username`: The username to authenticate with.

- `--password`: The password to authenticate with.

Assuming that you're testing with the `webauth` module that we just created, a basic `salt` command will look like this:

```
salt --auth=webauth --username=larry --password=123pass '*' test.ping
```

Testing with Salt API

You can also test `auth` modules using Salt API. This can be easily accomplished using the `curl` command that is commonly available in Linux. Before you can test using this method, you need to configure Salt API inside the `master` configuration file.

Please note that the following configuration block is insecure, as it does not use SSL. Never set `disable_ssl` to `True` in production! As a safety measure, this configuration block also sets Salt API to only listen to requests from the local host:

```
rest_cherrypy:
    port: 8080
    host: 127.0.0.1
    debug: True
    disable_ssl: True
```

Once you have Salt API configured, go ahead and start the `salt-master` and `salt-api` services in the foreground (in two different windows):

```
# salt-master -l debug
```

```
# salt-api -l debug
```

Use the following `curl` command to run the `test.ping` function:

```
# curl localhost:8080/run \
    -H 'Accept: application/json' \
    -d username=larry \
    -d password=123pass \
    -d eauth=pam \
    -d client=local \
    -d tgt='*' \
    -d fun='test.ping'
```

The most important arguments here are `eauth`, which is equivalent to the `--auth` parameter from the `salt` command, and `client`, which specifies which type of module to access. Here, we use `local`, which refers to execution modules. Some of the other available arguments are `runner` and `wheel`, for runner and wheel modules.

When you issue the preceding command with the correct credentials, you will receive a JSON string back with the result:

```
{"return": [{"dufresne": true}]}
```

If you issue it with bad credentials, you will receive an error page that includes the following text:

```
<h2>401 Unauthorized</h2>
<p>No permission -- see authorization schemes</p>
```

If you look at the window with `salt-master` running in the foreground, you will see an error message like this:

```
[WARNING ] Authentication failure of type "eauth" occurred for user
larry.
```

And if you look in the window running `salt-api`, you will see a message like this:

```
127.0.0.1 - - [26/Jan/2016:08:25:32] "POST /run HTTP/1.1" 401 1214 ""
"curl/7.46.0"
[INFO    ] 127.0.0.1 - - [26/Jan/2016:08:25:32] "POST /run HTTP/1.1" 401
1214 "" "curl/7.46.0"
```

Managing the Master with the wheel modules

The wheel system is designed to provide an API to the Master, which is accessible via programs that give external access to the Master, such as Salt API.

One of the first things that you'll find when writing wheel modules is that there is no command-line program available for testing wheel modules directly. Wheel modules generally include functionality that would be available via some other means, were you logged directly in to the Master, but are still useful when manual access is not an option.

For instance, possibly the most commonly used wheel module is key, which allows a programmatic way to manage Minion keys without using the key command. Because wheel modules are available to the reactor system, you can write reactor modules that can automatically accept or delete keys for Minions based on predefined conditions.

Wrapping a wheel around runners

For our example module, we'll put together a wheel module that returns a small amount of data concerning runner modules. This module is a simplified version of the runner functions inside the sys execution module. The reason these functions might be useful as a wheel module is that runners are designed to run on the Master, not Minions. If you do not run the salt-minion service on the Master, then you have no way to programmatically list available runner modules on the Master.

To start things off, we'll create a function that does nothing more than list all of the functions available in the runner system:

```
'''
Show information about runners on the Master

This file should be saved as salt/wheel/runners.py
'''
import salt.runner


def list_functions():
    '''
    List the functions for all runner modules.
    '''
    run_ = salt.runner.Runner(__opts__)
    return sorted(run_.functions)
```

This function doesn't do a whole lot. It sets up a connection to the Runner system and assigns it to a run_ object. Then it returns a sorted list of all of the runner functions available on the Master.

To test this, we'll need Salt API configured, just like we did in the *Troubleshooting external authentication* section. Then we issue a command that sets client to use the wheel system:

```
# curl localhost:8080/run \
    -H 'Accept: application/json' \
    -d username=larry \
    -d password=123pass \
    -d eauth=pam \
    -d client=wheel \
    -d fun='runners.list_functions'
```

On a Master that only has the manage module available, we would get a JSON string back that looks like this:

```
"return": [{"tag": "salt/wheel/20160126084725920013", "data": {"jid":
"20160126084725920013", "return": ["manage.alived", "manage.allowed",
"manage.bootstrap", "manage.bootstrap_psexec", "manage.down", "manage.
get_stats", "manage.joined", "manage.key_regen", "manage.lane_stats",
"manage.list_not_state", "manage.list_state", "manage.not_alived",
"manage.not_allowed", "manage.not_joined", "manage.not_present",
"manage.not_reaped", "manage.present", "manage.reaped", "manage.
road_stats", "manage.safe_accept", "manage.status", "manage.tagify",
"manage.up", "manage.versions"], "success": true, "_stamp": "2016-01-
26T15:47:25.974625", "tag": "salt/wheel/20160126084725920013", "user":
"larry", "fun": "wheel.runners.list_functions"}}]}
```

Let's go ahead and build on that a little bit and add a runner-specific version of the sys.doc function in the execution modules:

```
from salt.utils.doc import strip_rst as _strip_rst


def doc():
    '''
    Return the docstrings for all runners.
    '''
    run_ = salt.runner.Runner(__opts__)
    docs = {}
    for fun in run_.functions:
        docs[fun] = run_.functions[fun].__doc__
    return _strip_rst(docs)
```

Once again, this function sets up a connection to the Runner system, and assigns it to the run_ object. It then iterates through the functions inside the run_ object, extracting the docstrings that live inside the __doc__ attribute. Each docstring is added to a docs dictionary, which is passed through a function in Salt called _strip_rst(), which cleans things up a little bit.

Let's finish things up with a function that lists just the runner modules available, but no other information about them such as docstrings or even function names:

```
__func_alias__ = {
    'list_': 'list'
}


def list_():
    '''
```

```
List the runners loaded on the minion
'''
run_ = salt.runner.Runner(__opts__)
runners = set()
for func in run_.functions:
    comps = func.split('.')
    if len(comps) < 2:
        continue
    runners.add(comps[0])
return sorted(runners)
```

This function expands upon the `list_runners()` function by stripping out function names and adding the resulting module names to a set called `runners`. As before, a sorted copy of that set is returned.

The final wheel module

With all of our functions put together, we will end up with a cohesive module that looks like this:

```
'''
Show information about runners on the Master

This file should be saved as salt/wheel/runners.py
'''
import salt.runner
from salt.utils.doc import strip_rst as _strip_rst

__func_alias__ = {
    'list_': 'list'
}


def doc():
    '''
    Return the docstrings for all runners.
    '''
    run_ = salt.runner.Runner(__opts__)
    docs = {}
    for fun in run_.functions:
        docs[fun] = run_.functions[fun].__doc__
    return _strip_rst(docs)
```

```
def list_():
    '''
    List the runners loaded on the minion
    '''
    run_ = salt.runner.Runner(__opts__)
    runners = set()
    for func in run_.functions:
        comps = func.split('.')
        if len(comps) < 2:
            continue
        runners.add(comps[0])
    return sorted(runners)


def list_functions():
    '''
    List the functions for all runner modules.
    '''
    run_ = salt.runner.Runner(__opts__)
    return sorted(run_.functions)
```

Troubleshooting wheel modules

Once again, wheel modules are a little special when it comes to troubleshooting, because there is no specific command-line program in Salt that executes them directly. Unlike `auth` modules, they can't even be tested using the `salt` command.

However, as you have just seen, they can be tested using Salt API and `curl`:

```
# curl localhost:8080/run \
    -H 'Accept: application/json' \
    -d username=larry \
    -d password=123pass \
    -d eauth=pam \
    -d client=wheel \
    -d fun='runners.list'
```

You can also test wheel modules using the event system in Salt. It is good to get used to testing this way, since wheel modules are so useful inside reactor modules.

Let's go ahead and set up a reactor that deletes a Minion's key from the Master:

```
# This reactor should be saved as /srv/reactor/test_delete.sls
test_delete_minion:
  wheel.key.delete:
    - match: data['bad_minion']
```

Then add that reactor to the `master` configuration file:

```
reactor:
  - 'user/minon/delete/*':
    - '/srv/reactor/test_delete.sls'
```

Go ahead and create a bad Minion key on the Master:

```
# touch /etc/salt/pki/master/minions/ronald
```

After restarting the Master, go ahead and issue a command to trigger the reactor:

```
# salt myminion event.fire_master '{"bad_minion":"ronald"}' 'user/minion/
delete/ronald'
```

Once you issue this command, you can use the `salt-key` command to make sure that the Minion's bad key is no longer there:

```
# salt-key -L
```

Or for bonus points, why not use Salt API to make sure that Minion's key is gone?:

```
# curl localhost:8080/run \
    -H 'Accept: application/json' \
    -d username=larry \
    -d password=123pass \
    -d eauth=pam \
    -d client=wheel \
    -d fun='key.list' \
    -d match='ronald'
```

```
{"return": [{"tag": "salt/wheel/20160126091522567932", "data": {"jid":
"20160126091522567932", "return": {}, "success": true, "_stamp": "2016-
01-26T16:15:22.576966", "tag": "salt/wheel/20160126091522567932", "user":
"larry", "fun": "wheel.key.list"}}]}
```

Don't be fooled by the fact that `success` is set to `true`; the important value here is `return`, which is an empty dictionary.

Summary

External authentication (or auth) modules allow an external authentication system to validate user credentials on the Master. This can be used for authenticating a user locally, but it is required for using external systems that connect to Salt.

Wheel modules allow API access to Master-side functionality. The functions contained in a wheel module generally allow the management of features that are normally available via some other means on the Master locally, but not other means from an external endpoint outside the Master. However, wheel modules can contain any Master-side management that you deem necessary.

Congratulations! You made it all the way through Extending SaltStack! We've included a couple of appendices to give you some general development guidelines and some information about contributing to the community.

As you can see, there is a world of Salt development to explore. More modules are added regularly, and occasionally new types of modules will appear as well. While we haven't covered everything there is or will be, you now have a solid foundation that you can use to tackle new Salt code as you come across it. Good luck out there; I hope you win!

A
Connecting Different Modules

When building an infrastructure, it is helpful to understand how each of the module types fits together. This includes both how they fit together inside of Salt and how you are able to use those connections to build your own solutions.

Separating Master and Minion functionality

It's easy to think of Salt in terms of the following: the Master sends commands to the Minions, the Minions do the work, and then the Minions send the results back to the Master. However, the Master and the Minion are two distinct components that work together in harmony to complete their respective tasks.

It is important to keep in mind that when the Minion is running in a Masterless mode (using `salt-call --local`), it behaves as its own Master, and outside of a few specific features (such as `salt-key` and runners that make use of `local_client`), any feature that is available on the Master is also available on the Minion, using the same configuration options that would appear in the `master` file, but in the `minion` file instead.

But when running with a Master and one or more Minions, they are two distinct entities. Some module types are available to either the Master or the Minion; there are many more that are only available for that specific service.

Let us have a look at a diagrammatic representation of the Salt Master topology:

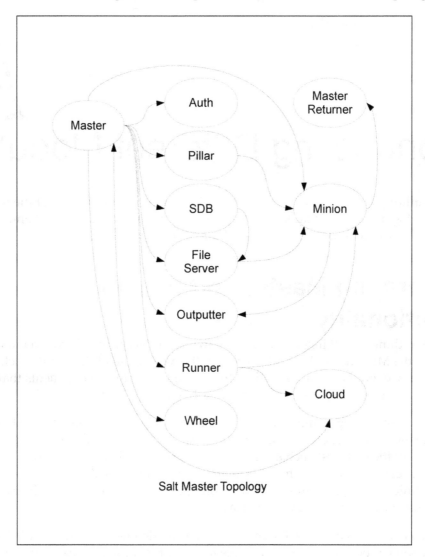

Salt Master Topology

And now follows the diagrammatic representation of the Salt Minion topology:

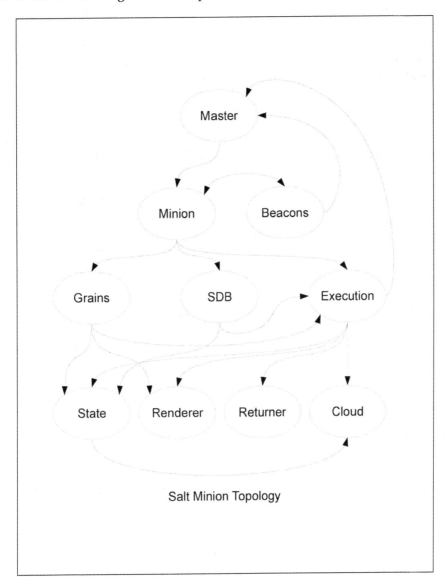

Salt Minion Topology

Like the Master and the Minion, each module type is specific and distinct. However, like the Master and the Minion, modules connect to each other and work in concert to accomplish larger workflows. Regardless of module type, the Master and the Minion will always communicate directly (using transport modules, which are beyond the scope of this book). Beyond that, different modules are able to communicate with each other to varying degrees.

The Master generally uses its own modules directly. Some of those modules may be used to provide Minions with resources (such as file server modules), but a number of them are used entirely for providing resources to the Master itself. Master returners are functionally identical to returners that execute on the Minion, with the exception of how they get their data.

Minion modules communicate with each other extensively. Execution modules can pull data from grain and SDB modules (and from pillars, through the Master) and cross-call each other. State modules are themselves called from an execution module, but also have access to cross-callback to execution modules. Renderers are used by a number of different module types, and when all is said and done, returners transport return data to the correct destination.

Salt Cloud is the odd man out, because while it can be accessed via either a runner or an execution module, it can also be accessed directly, and even used independently of the rest of Salt. In fact, it can be used to manage nodes without even installing Salt on them.

Working with dunders

For those of you not in the know, *dunder* refers to a variable that is preceded and succeeded by two underscores. For instance, one of the most common dunders in Salt is `__opts__`, which contains the configuration for either the Master or the Minion, depending on the context. There are a number of dunders that work together to form the glue that ties all of Salt together. Let's take a look at them in turn:

- `__opts__`: On a Master, the `__opts__` dictionary contains a composite of the information located in the Master's configuration files (normally `/etc/salt/master` plus files located in the `/etc/salt/master.d/` directory), along with the default values for configuration parameters not specified, plus any internal configuration that Salt generates for its own use at runtime.

On a Minion, `__opts__` contains the same sort of information (but from the `/etc/salt/minion` file and the `/etc/salt/minion.d/` directory), when it is connected to the Master. However, when the Minion is used in a Masterless mode (such as when called from `salt-call --local`), any defaults are filled in as if it were a Master, rather than a Minion. This is because lookups such as pillars and files need to be provided from a Master of some sort, and in this capacity the Minion needs to play that role.

- `__salt__`: In modules that run on the Minions (most notably execution and state modules), `__salt__` contains a list of function calls to all of the available execution modules on the system. These items can be called directly, as if they were functions inside the calling module itself. For example:

```
__salt__['disk.usage']()
__salt__['cmd.run']('ls -l /')
__salt__['cmd.run']('dir c:\\')
```

Using a function in this way is referred to as *cross-calling*. Because it calls out to execution modules, which are only available as a Minion, the Master does not make use of cross-calling.

- `__grains__`: Another Minion-only dunder is the `__grains__` dictionary, which contains a copy of all of the grains computed for the Minion. This is used extensively throughout Salt to help Minions auto-detect what kinds of resources are available. It is possible to start `salt-call` without detecting grains by passing the `--skip-grains` flag, like this:

```
# salt-call --local --skip-grains test.ping
```

You will notice that if you try this, the Minion responds much more quickly. But if you try to use any modules much more advanced than `test`, you will quickly find out how important grains are to the functionality of the Minion.

- `__pillar__`: Pillars have their own dunder dictionary as well, whose name is strangely singular (`__pillar__` instead of `__pillars__`). Unlike grains, which are generated by the Minion, pillars are generated by the Master. However, if you run `salt-call` in `--local` mode like this, you will discover that as `__opts__` now contains Master-side configuration, pillar configuration that would normally live on the Master will now be accepted by the Minion:

```
# salt-call --local test.ping
```

- This is incredibly useful for writing and debugging pillar modules, since you don't run the risk of contaminating other Minions with bad pillar data.

- `__context__`: This dictionary is available both to state and execution modules. When Salt fires up the first execution module (which will be the `state` module on a state run), it creates the `__context__` dictionary. All of the information entered into this dictionary will persist across each subsequent module, so that different modules have a means of storing information for later use by another module. Once the final module has finished, the `__context__` dictionary will be destroyed.

  Make sure that if you decide to use `__context__`, you check for the existence of keys in it before trying to set or use them. This is because you really have no way of knowing beforehand which order somebody will use modules in, so you shouldn't assume that things have or have not been populated.

 For more information about Salt dunders, check out:
`https://docs.saltstack.com/en/latest/topics/development/dunder_dictionaries.html`

Using the event bus

The event bus does not appear in the topology drawings because it is available anywhere inside of Salt, just by importing the `salt.event` library. It also has the ability to call out to other module types, using the reactor system. Reactors have access to execution, state, and runner modules.

 You may be wondering why we didn't cover reactor modules in this book. In truth, there is no such thing as a reactor module. Reactors are written using standard SLS files, which can include extra functionality using the renderer system. For more thorough discussions on writing and using reactors, be sure to check out *Mastering SaltStack, Joseph Hall, Packt Publishing*.

Because the event bus is so ubiquitous, it can be a very powerful tool for tying together the other module types into a cohesive workflow.

For example, let's take a look at Salt Cloud. It can be operated independently from the rest of Salt, but when using a Master + Minions setup, it will fire events to the Master during the creation and deletion process that can be picked up by reactors.

Salt Cloud events use tags that are namespaced in a way that can be easily determined by reactors:

```
salt/cloud/<minion_id>/<operation>
```

Available events vary depending on the cloud provider, and the work that provider has been configured to do, but a properly written cloud driver will always fire at least these two events when creating a node:

```
salt/cloud/<minion_id>/creating
salt/cloud/<minion_id>/created
```

It will also fire these two events when deleting a node:

```
salt/cloud/<minion_id>/deleting
salt/cloud/<minion_id>/deleted
```

Operations that perform maintenance on Minions and their resources can be kicked off using these events. For instance, if you want to sync a Minion's resources as soon as it's created, you can use a reactor that looks like:

```
sync_minion:
  cmd.saltutil.sync_all:
    - tgt: data['id']
```

Because a Minion will be available by the time Salt Cloud sends the `salt/cloud/<minion_id>/created` tag, you can set a reactor to ensure that the Minion is synced as soon as it comes online, without having to configure any `startup_states`.

Firing events

You can fire events both from the Minion-side modules (such as execution and state modules) and Master-side modules (such as runners). From a Minion-side module, you need nothing more than to call out to the event execution module as follows:

```
__salt__['event.fire_master'](data_dict, some_tag)
```

But in Master-side modules, you need to do a little more work, since `__salt__` isn't available. You need to import `salt.utils.event`, then use it to fire the event. This isn't much more work, but you do have to do some setup. It looks like:

```
import os.path
import salt.utils.event
import salt.syspaths
sock_dir = os.path.join(salt.syspaths.SOCK_DIR, 'master')
transport = __opts__.get('transport', 'zeromq')
event = salt.utils.event.get_event(
    'master',
    sock_dir,
```

```
        transport,
        listen=False,
    )
    event.fire_event(data_dict, some_tag)
```

Let's go over what happened here. First, we set up our imports. The `salt.syspaths` library contains information about where standard files and directories will be located on this system. In our case, we need to connect to a socket called `master`. We use this information to set up a variable called `sock_dir`, which tells Salt where to find the event bus to connect to.

We also find out which transport mechanism is configured for this system. This will usually be `zeromq`, but it can also be another protocol such as `raet` or `tcp`. Then we set up an object using the `get_event()` function. The first argument says which bus we're dealing with, then the `sock_dir`, transport, and finally we say that we're not going to be listening for events' we'll be sending them.

> What do we mean by *which bus we're dealing with*? Both the Master and the Minion have their own event bus. A Minion can either fire a message to itself using the `minion` bus, or to the Master using the `master` bus. The Minion event bus is rarely used except by the internal Salt code, but the Master bus is used extensively.

Once we have the event object set up, we can fire the event. The data (which can be a list or a dictionary) is specified first, and then the event tag. If you like, you can set up a listener on the Master to see those events come in:

```
# salt-run state.event pretty=True
```

One of the most useful things that events are used in is reactors. As mentioned earlier, for more information on writing reactors, check out *Mastering SaltStack, Joseph Hall, Packt Publishing*.

B
Contributing Code Upstream

A number of users have commented over the years that Salt has a low barrier to entry for new developers. This can be attributed in part both to the friendly and professional community, and the tools that are used to manage the Salt code base.

How the community works

The Salt community comprises users and developers from all over the globe. The vast majority of these people are professionals who use Salt in a business environment, though some hobbyists have found their place among the ranks too.

When most people make their way to the community, they are looking for help and information about a particular situation that they are working with. This may be as minor as looking for examples or documentation, or it could be more serious, such as reporting what appears to be a bug in the software.

Once people have spent some time in the community, they often stick around to help out other users. Remember that while some of them may be experts with Salt and the various pieces of technology that it manages, they are still just users like you, who are contributing their own time to help out people like you.

Asking questions and reporting issues

There are three primary places where the Salt community gets together to discuss the software and help each other out: the mailing list, the IRC chat room, and the issue tracker on GitHub.

There are three types of messages that you will generally find in these places: questions about the software, bug reports, and feature requests. In general, questions about the software should be asked either on the mailing list or in IRC. Bug reports and feature requests are better suited to the issue tracker.

Using the mailing list

The salt-users mailing list is a very active discussion environment, hosted on Google Groups. The mailing list can be found at:

```
https://groups.google.com/d/forum/salt-users
```

You can browse the mailing list at the preceding link, or you can set up an e-mail subscription and get messages sent to your inbox, where you can reply to them. There are, typically, a good dozen or so e-mails a day, so if that sounds like too many, then maybe just looking online is the way to go.

If you're going to post a question, there are a few guidelines that will help you out:

- When you ask a question, try to post enough information about your problem so that people will be able help you out. In the past, people have asked how to fix a particular problem without stating what the problem actually is, or in some cases, even the part of Salt that the question pertains to. As you can imagine, this isn't helpful to anybody.

- Describe what you're trying to do, and what you expect to happen. If something isn't working the way that you expect, make sure to state what is actually happening.

- You may need to post the output from a command in order to explain what is happening. If this is the case, make sure to post the actual command that you're running, and the relevant part of the output. If you issue a command that results in dozens of lines of logging output, but the actual error only takes up five lines, then just post those five lines to start with. If somebody asks for more, then go ahead and post more.

 Be careful when posting logs and configuration files! All too often, people will accidentally post an API key, password, or private network information without meaning to. Before pasting any information at a place online, where somebody can see it, make sure to remove any sensitive information. Making sure not to post long log messages will make this a lot easier.

- It is also helpful to know which version of Salt you are running. It is likely that your particular experience is unique to a specific version of Salt. Rather than just saying which version of Salt, it is often more helpful to give the output of the following command:

```
# salt --versions-report
```

- If you are working with Salt Cloud, then make sure to get that report instead, using:

```
# salt-cloud --versions-report
```

- Because Salt Cloud uses a different set of libraries, using its `versions` report will give more information that may be useful, in addition to all of the version information for Salt itself.

- If you happen to find the resolution for your situation from outside the mailing list, it is also a good idea to reply to your own thread with a copy of the solution. The mailing list is archived on Google's servers, and if somebody else with your issue searches for it, they will appreciate seeing the solution. Believe me, few things are more frustrating than finding a dozen different people asking the same question on a dozen different mailing lists, with either no solution or a message from the original person saying, "Hey, I figured it out," and leaving it at that.

Using IRC

IRC, or Internet relay chat, is a type of chat room that's been around for a very long time. If you already have an IRC client, you can connect to the Freenode server at:

```
irc.freenode.com
```

And then join the Salt chat room at:

```
#salt
```

If you don't have an IRC client yet, you might want to consider Pidgin, which is a chat client that supports a number of chat protocols. It's not the most popular IRC client by any means, but it's easy to use and available for Windows, Mac, and Linux. You can download it at:

```
https://www.pidgin.im/
```

If you don't want to commit to an IRC client, Freenode does have a web-based IRC client that you can use to connect to Salt's chat room. You can find this client at:

```
https://webchat.freenode.net/
```

When you connect to Salt's chat room, there are a few things that will be useful to know:

- **Be patient.** There are hundreds of people logged in to the Salt chat room at any given time, but not all of them are actively participating. It is very common for people to log in to an IRC room while at work, and check it periodically throughout the day. When you ask a question, don't expect an immediate answer. Somebody may be watching at that moment and try to help you, but it may take an hour for the right person to see your question and jump in to try to answer it.

- **Be ready to provide information as necessary.** The kind person who offers to help you may ask for log messages or code snippets, or may ask you to try a few different commands, and post the response.

  You may want to look into getting an account on a text-sharing service. One such popular service is PasteBin:

  `http://pastebin.com/`

  However, you might also want to look into using GitHub's gist service:

  `https://gist.github.com/`

  This has become an increasingly popular way to share logs and code snippets as with PasteBin, but with the kind of revision management that Git is known for.

- **Post solutions.** As with the mailing list, conversations in the Salt chat room are archived. You can find them at:

  `https://irclog.perlgeek.de/salt/`

  If you find the solution as you are working on the problem, and it's not obvious by looking at the conversation what it is, make sure to post it in the chat room so that others can find it later.

Using the issue tracker

When you come across a situation that you know is a bug, or you have a feature request, the Salt issue tracker on GitHub is the way to go. You can find it at:

`https://github.com/saltstack/salt/issues`

You may come across a situation where you don't know whether your problem is the result of inexperience, or an actual bug. If you're not sure, go ahead and post it on the mailing list. If it is a bug, then you will probably be asked to file an issue in the issue tracker, assuming somebody else hasn't already filed the same issue.

One of the advantages of filing an issue in the issue tracker is that you are automatically subscribed to updates for that issue. That means that when others post questions and comments on the issue, you will receive an e-mail with a copy of their response. If somebody else posted the issue, then you can still subscribe to it. Just look for the **Subscribe** button on the right-hand side of the issue page:

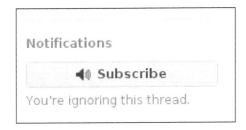

Once you hit that button, it will change to say **Unsubscribe**. If you ever get tired of receiving updates for that issue (even if you created it), then you can unsubscribe from it. But if you've left comments, I would encourage you to remain subscribed, in case anybody wants to ask you further questions down the road.

Once again, make sure to post any relevant information, exactly as you would on the mailing list. Detailed information about the issue, version reports, and code snippets are all helpful. A very recent addition to the Salt issue tracker is the use of templates, which provide reminders as to which information to give.

Using GitHub markdown

One incredibly helpful feature in GitHub is the ability to use markdown. You can find a helpful guide to markdown at:

```
https://guides.github.com/features/mastering-markdown/
```

By far the most useful markdown syntax to know is how to mark out code blocks. The character used to mark out code is commonly known as the **backtick**, also known as the grave accent. On an American QWERTY keyboard, this key is located in the top-left position:

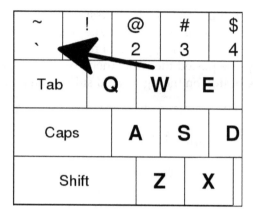

When you place a single backtick in front of a piece of text and another at the end, then the text will be formatted as a piece of code. If you need to format multiple lines, then start with three backticks together on the first line, and three more together on the last line. Blocking out code this way helps immensely with readability.

Write Preview	Write Preview
This sentence includes `inline code`. ```	This sentence includes `inline code` .
This entire block will be formatted as code. ```	This entire block will be formatted as code.

Understanding the Salt Style Guide

If you've spent enough time in Python, then you're already familiar with the Style Guide for Python Code, also known as PEP 8. For those who have not seen it, or if you need a refresher, you can take a look at it here:

```
https://www.python.org/dev/peps/pep-0008/
```

There is also a guide to the Salt Coding Style, available at:

```
https://docs.saltstack.com/en/latest/topics/development/conventions/
style.html
```

In general, Salt coding conventions follow PEP 8, but there are some key differences:

- **Quoting:** One of the first conventions that new developers come across is that Salt uses single quotes (') instead of double quotes ("). This applies to everything from string formatting to docstrings.

- **Line length:** It is very common for code to restrict lines to no longer than 80 characters. This seems to be especially adhered to in Python, but it is based on an older convention where computer screens were exactly 80 characters wide. Because this is no longer the case, it is considered acceptable in Salt to expand to 120 characters, particularly if it helps with readability.

- **Tabs versus spaces:** Salt uses four spaces for indentation. No tabs. No exceptions.

Using Pylint

Salt makes extensive use of a program called **Pylint** to ensure that its code adheres to its style guide. You can find information about installing Pylint at:

```
http://www.pylint.org/
```

Keep in mind that Salt currently uses Python 2 (the minimum version being 2.6), so if you're working in a distribution where both Python 2 and 3 versions of Pylint are available, make sure you use the Python 2 version.

The Salt code base ships with a `.pylintrc` file to be used with Pylint. It doesn't get used by default, so you need to make sure to point it out to Pylint:

```
$ cd /path/to/salt
$ pylint --rcfile=.pylintrc
```

Not only will this file allow you to check your code against Salt style guidelines but also to check the entire code base at once. This is important, because the loader inserts variables into modules that wouldn't be picked up otherwise by Pylint.

Creating pull requests on GitHub

Whereas many project communities accept code only through mailing lists or complex websites, Salt has opted to stick with pull requests for accepting code contributions. A list of active pull requests can be found at:

```
https://github.com/saltstack/salt/pulls
```

The complete details of using Git are way beyond the scope of this book, but it is worth going over the steps to clone the Salt repository and put in a new pull request.

First, you will need your own fork of Salt on GitHub. If you don't have one yet, then use the **Fork** button at Salt's own GitHub page:

```
https://github.com/saltstack/salt
```

Assuming that your GitHub username is *mygithubuser*, your new fork will appear at:

```
https://github.com/mygithubuser/salt
```

Once you have a fork set up, you'll need to clone a copy to your computer. The following steps assume that you work in a command-line environment, such as Linux:

1. If you have an SSH key set up, you can clone using SSH:

   ```
   $ git clone git@github.com:mygithubuser/salt.git
   ```

   Otherwise, you'll need to clone over HTTPS:

   ```
   $ git clone https://github.com/mygithubuser/salt.git
   ```

2. You will also need to add the original SaltStack repository to your local clone, to be able to create pull requests:

   ```
   $ git remote add upstream
   https://github.com/saltstack/salt.git
   ```

3. The default Git branch is `develop`. If you're adding a new feature to Salt, the work should be performed on a branch based on `develop`. To create a new branch called `newfeature` and switch to it, use:

   ```
   $ git checkout -b newfeature
   ```

4. When you are ready to put in a pull request, it is best to rebase your branch to make sure it doesn't conflict with any other pull requests that have been merged since your last update:

```
$ git checkout develop
$ git fetch upstream
$ git pull upstream develop
$ git checkout newfeature
$ git rebase develop
```

 For more information on using rebase, check out:
https://help.github.com/articles/using-git-rebase/

5. Once you have rebased, go ahead and push your branch up to GitHub:

```
$ git push origin newfeature
```

6. When you visit your fork on GitHub again, you will see a link that says **New Pull Request**. From there, you can look at the diff readout between your branch and the current version of the develop branch on GitHub, and create your pull request when you're satisfied with it.

As with issue submission, pull requests now also have a template to use as a guide to provide useful information about describing the changes that your pull request includes.

Using other branches

If you're submitting bug fixes, then it may be more appropriate to submit them against a branch that matches a specific version of Salt. If you know which version of Salt the bug was first found in, then use that branch. The exception would be if the branch in question is so old that it is no longer being maintained. If that is the case, then choose the oldest branch that is being maintained. For instance, if the oldest maintained version is 2015.8.x, then check out the 2015.8 branch:

```
$ git checkout 2015.8
```

Understanding test errors in pull requests

When you submit a new pull request, GitHub will trigger the test suite to run against it. This will take several minutes, as it needs to create a new virtual machine, and start a lint test using Pylint, as well as tests on popular platforms such as CentOS and Ubuntu:

As the tests are running, you can check progress by clicking the **Details** button on the right:

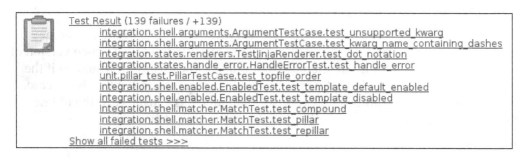

Click on one of the tests to see more information. You will see output such as error messages, stacktraces, and standard output and standard error output.

There is a chance that one or more of the test failures that show up in your pull request are not actually your fault. It could be that another pull request was merged, which caused unforeseen issues on the build server. If the errors that show up don't look to be related to your code, leave a comment to ask about it. One of the core developers at SaltStack will see it and help you out.

Lint errors look a little different. When you look at the details for a lint test, you will see a list of files that are affected. Click on one, and you will see each error marked out. Hover over it to find out what went wrong:

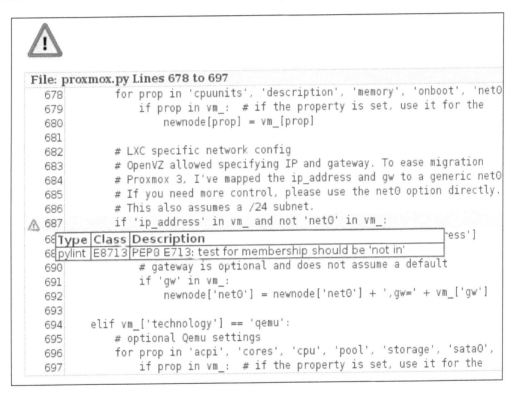

If you would like more information about the lint test, you can click on **Console Output** on the left, to see a full log of the lint test.

Once you have made corrections to the code in your local Git clone, commit them as you normally would, and push them back up to GitHub:

```
$ git push origin newfeature
```

A new test run will be scheduled, and any remaining errors will show up as before. Once all of the errors have been resolved, a core developer will be able to merge your code.

Index

troubleshooting 180
using 177
external job cache
versus Master job cache 86
external pillars
adding 35-37
another external pillar 37-40
configuring 34
creating 34

F

file formats
about 69
data serializing 70
render pipes, using 70, 71
templates, working with 70
files
used, by Salt 111, 112
file servers
troubleshooting 132
filesystem
mimicking 112
final beacon module 173
final cloud module
defining 156
final module
about 21, 90
defining 125
first returner 83
Freenode
URL 201
function
about 154
defining 113
dir_list() 116-118
envs() 116
file_hash() 122-125
file_list() 116-118
find_file() 118
module, setting up 113-115
serve_file() 119
update() 120-122
using 156

G

generic cloud module
_query() function, setting up 142-145
actions, using 154
functions, using 154
http.query(), using 140
nodes, listing 147
profile details, obtaining 145
required configuration, checking 138-140
REST API, defining 141
VM, creating 149-153
VM, destroying 153, 154
writing 138
gist service, GitHub
URL 202
GitHub
pull requests, creating on 206, 207
GitHub markdown
URL 203
grains and pillars, troubleshooting
about 40
dynamic grains not showing up 40
external pillars not showing up 40
grains, setting dynamically
about 29
basic grains, setting 29-32
execution modules, defining 33
final grains module 33

H

HTTP service checking, example
about 60
another stateful function 63, 66
credentials, checking 60, 61
first stateful function 61-63

I

IRC
URL 201
issue tracker, Salt
URL 203

J

job caches
  using 84-90

K

kwargs 155

L

Libcloud
  about 137
  advantages 137
  disadvantages 137
loader system
  extending 3-5
local client
  different targets, using 100, 101
  final module 106
  jobs, combining 101-105
  scripting with 98-100
  using 97, 98

M

Master
  and Minion functionality,
      separating 191-194
  managing, with wheel modules 183
modules
  loading, with Python 5
modules, loader system
  about 3
  Beacons 4
  cloud modules 4
  engines 4
  execution modules 3
  external authentication modules 4
  external file server modules 4
  grain modules 3
  Master Tops system 4
  outputter modules 4
  pillar modules 4
  pkgdb module 5

pkgfile module 5
  proxy minion modules 4
  queue modules 4
  renderer modules 4
  returner modules 4
  roster modules 4
  runner modules 4
  SDB modules 4
  state modules 4
  wheel modules 4
modules, with Python
  detection methods, using 6
  grains, detecting 5
module types
  external authentication modules 177
  wheel modules 177

N

nodes
  full node data, querying 148
  listing 147
  standard node data, querying 147
nspawn
  URL 168

O

outputter modules
  output, pickling 94, 95
  writing 94
outputters
  troubleshooting 95

P

Paramiko 115
PasteBin
  URL 202
Pidgin
  URL 201
plugins
  lazy loading modules 3
  modules, loading 2
  standard modules 2

www.ingramcontent.com/pod-product-compliance
Lightning Source LLC
Chambersburg PA
CBHW060546060326
40690CB00017B/3617